more than enough

Encountering El Shaddai

Vicki Jamison-Peterson

Vicki Jamison-Peterson Ministries
P.O. Box 700030
Tulsa, Oklahoma 74170

Unless otherwise noted, all Scripture quotations are from The New King James Version, Copyright © 1979, 1980, 1982, Thomas Nelson Inc., Publishers. Used by permission.

Scripture quotations marked kjv are taken from the King James Version of the Bible.

Cover Design by: Chuck Fowler

More than Enough
Encountering El Shaddai

ISBN: 978-0-88144-341-7

Copyright © 1983 & 1990 by
Vicki Jamison-Peterson Ministries
P.O. Box 700030
Tulsa, OK 74170
www.vjpm.org

Published by
THORNCROWN PUBLISHING
A division of Yorkshire Publishing Group
7707 East 111th, Suite 104
Tulsa, Oklahoma 74133
www.yorkshirepublishing.com

Printed in the United States of America. All rights reserved under International Copyright Law. Contents and/or cover may not be reproduced in whole or in part in any form without the express written consent of the Author.

contents

INTRODUCTION 5

chapter one
✓ "I Am El Shaddai"..11
Workbook..166

chapter two
✓ More Than Enough For Your Salvation 31
Workbook..169

chapter three
✓ More Than Enough For Your Inner Power..................................43
Workbook..173

chapter four
✓ More Than Enough For Your Healing 57
Workbook..177

chapter five
✓ More Than Enough For Your Family..69
Workbook..180

Her Life, Her Love, Her Legacy..85

chapter six
✓ More Than Enough For Your Finances......................................101
Workbook..184

chapter seven
More Than Enough For Your Weaknesses 115
Workbook..187

chapter eight
More Than Enough For Your Circumstances 127
Workbook..190

chapter nine
More Than Enough For Your Every Need 141
Workbook...194

chapter ten
Releasing The Power of El Shaddai 149
Workbook...197

introduction

I SAW HIM WHEN I was 3 years old!

It's still as vivid, as clear in my memory as if it happened yesterday. I was in the backyard of my home in Marlin, Texas. Someone had lifted me out of the sandbox and set me up in a small tree. I sat on that branch and looked up into the sky.

My friends had told me that if I looked into the sky I could see God. So that was my pastime—looking for God. Every day I would look up into the sky and scan from horizon to horizon. I wanted to see Him.

And I did. One day I looked beyond the white, pillow-soft clouds ... beyond the vast blueness of the sky that reached out forever in all directions ... and I "saw" God.

At the age of 3, I experienced an electric moment of awareness of who God was ... of what He was. I didn't have the words to describe what I sensed, what I *knew* deep inside me. This God was more than the God of my Bible storybooks ... more than the God of my bedtime prayers.

The reality of this God who was *more* was planted deep within my being. It was like a seed within me, waiting to break through the surface of my life—to grow and blossom and become fruitful.

It was like there was a homing device within me, drawing me, steering me toward the time and place when a glorious experience could occur—when my conscious mind would fully register what my subconscious and my spirit were trying to get through to me.

No matter what my life became from that moment on—good, bad, indifferent—I never forgot that dramatic, exciting, visionary glimpse I had of God when I was only 3. My spirit was exceptionally strong and tuned in.

But as I grew older, my head kept hearing what my spirit couldn't agree with. The God I heard about at church and from the people around me was not the God I had seen. My early religious background had all the usual negative overtones—but I never believed them. Yet, there was no one to talk to about what I *knew* inside me, and I didn't know how to articulate what I felt.

I had a conversion experience. I sought—and received—the baptism in the Holy Spirit. But the personal joy I found in those deeply moving experiences gradually lost its intensity amid the utter drabness of my religious environment. What I saw in church, in religious life, bored me. By the time I reached my mid-20s, I was almost convinced that Christians were all very dull and very boring.

I didn't think it should be that way, but I had nothing to enlarge my frame of reference. Life had no meaning. The religion I practiced was totally unsatisfying. I didn't have any spiritual freedom. The stern, forbidding deity of the religious people I knew was not appealing to me. And I didn't like the idea of being a pawn to be moved and acted upon by this cold, unloving, impersonal force in the universe.

Frankly, I lost interest. I honestly didn't care if my life went on any longer. When I found myself in the hospital facing a serious, life-threatening condition

introduction

that required major surgery, it really didn't matter to me if I lived or died. The doctors felt there was a possibility that I had cancer. One of my ovaries was greatly enlarged by a tumorous growth. There were large lumps on my back on each side of the spine. My friends were concerned. But I could have cared less. The night before the operation, I finally prayed—and that short prayer was a turning point in my life.

I said, "God, if You want me to live, I'll live my life for You. But if You don't, I'd just as soon go."

I wasn't aware that anything happened, but the growth in my ovary disappeared overnight. The next day the surgeons couldn't find it. The lumps in my back were there, but they were not malignant.

When I awoke after the operation, Mother said, "Vicki, we don't know what happened, but ..." and she told me. I said in my heart, "It was God!"

You see, from the moment I prayed that prayer, God began leading me.

After I was out of the hospital, I went to a church where there was an old prophetess named Clara Grace. And her message was revolutionary to me. She got up and talked about the reality of a God who talks to you. And instantly I knew what she was talking about ... I understood that was the God I'd become acquainted with when I was 3 years old.

I went out with this saintly woman later, and she began to open up and teach me many deep spiritual truths. *It was exciting* ... because everything she told me struck a responsive chord deep within me. I already *knew* everything she said, but I'd never been able to express those truths before ... to find the words to describe what I instinctively sensed inside.

It was wonderful! Because I was like a person who'd never had a drink of water! Step by step I was led to a realization, to the all-consuming awareness of the God who is not limited by life or death ... not by anything.

Then Clara Grace told me about a man named Kenneth Hagin. She said he was a great man of God, a teacher I needed to hear. Within three months I was in one of his meetings. He came to speak at the Voice of Healing ministry (now known as Christ for the Nations), and I can remember my exact place ... the very seat I was in. Kenneth Hagin taught on his theme Scripture verse, Mark 11:23, and suddenly there was a spiritual explosion inside me.

"I knew it, I knew it, I knew it all the time," I said to myself. "God is good, God is what He said He was. HE'S MORE!"

I remember wanting everybody to discover the same truth I had found. Like the New Testament story of the woman at the well, I went out and told every friend I had, every member of my family, "You've got to come and hear!" I had known these truths for so long but hadn't had the vocabulary to express them. And I didn't want my friends and family to miss the opportunity to understand.

Since then, my understanding, my awareness, my knowledge of God has grown and grown and grown. God hasn't changed—He's still the infinite, vast, unlimited God I met when I was 3—but my finite mind has become merged with His divine mind. God and I can't separate ourselves anymore. And He is becoming more and More and MORE.

My whole life now is devoted to helping people discover the reality of God. Wherever I go, I find too many for whom God is as sterile and powerless as a cardboard cutout ... as unrealistic as a shadowy image in a darkened mirror ...

introduction

as dull and boring as a worn-out ritual. And I help them experience the powerful presence of the God who is greater than all telling.

And that is why I have written this book. I want to introduce you to the God who calls Himself the Almighty, the All-Sufficient One. I want you to sense that you are part of Him and that He is part of you—so you have full access to the unlimited resources of all that God is.

At first it may boggle your mind, but as we go step by step and look into every part of your life, you will begin to comprehend that this God is *more*— that if you can believe, He's ready to do it.

I want you to know and experience *El Shaddai*—the God of more than enough!

chapter one

"I Am El Shaddai"

THE FAMILY CAR STALLS ON a busy expressway and refuses to budge, no matter how long Dad grinds the starter ... or how many wires he jiggles under the hood. Before long the kids are stirring restlessly. Mom is asking, "What are we going to do?" And Dad is starting to worry about the huge semi-trucks coming so close in the rush-hour traffic that the car shakes as they pass.

Just then a tow truck slows and parks just in front of them. A man dressed in coveralls gets out and walks back to the car. "Hello, I'm a mechanic—do you need some help?"

It's Grandmother's birthday, and the whole family is helping her celebrate by going out to dinner and to a concert. Shortly before intermission, she nudges her daughter and whispers, "I don't feel well—please help me to the lobby." They start out, but before they reach the lounge area, the older woman faints and slumps to the floor. Helpful hands lift her to a chair, and curious onlookers begin to assemble. As the frightened, tearful daughter kneels beside her stricken mother, a man walks purposefully across the lobby and touches her shoulder. "I'm a doctor—would you like me to try and help the lady?"

The noises started just after midnight. At first the young woman tried to ignore what she heard, hoping it was just the wind … or even her imagination. After all, it was her first apartment, her first time to be out on her own alone. But then the noises were too loud and too unmistakable to ignore. Someone was trying to get in. She could hear the would-be intruder trying the door … then the window.

She reached a trembling hand to the phone and dialed the emergency number … asked the operator to send help. Then she waited—for what seemed an eternity.

The knock at the front door startled her … and her heart was pounding so loud she could hardly ask who was there. "We're the police, ma'am—we've come to check a report of a prowler." Looking through the peephole, she saw uniforms and badges. The help she needed had come.

From the beginning of time, God revealed Himself to mankind by appearing at the point of man's need. Almost invariably He identified Himself with a name that described a divine attribute or property man desperately needed at that point in time.

"I Am El Shaddai"

Unfortunately, much of the vivid descriptiveness of the Hebrew names of God are lost when translated into English. The words translated as Lord or God have a much richer, deeper meaning in the original language—particularly in their compound forms.

Theologians and language experts tell us that the Hebrew names of God not only identify the Supreme Being, but reveal and describe His nature, His properties and characteristics. The Rev. C.I. Scofield, author and compiler of the study aids and notes in the famed Scofield Reference Bible, declared: "This revelation of God by His names is invariably made in connection with some particular need of His people, and there can be no need of man to which these names do not answer as showing that man's true resource is in God."

You see, the family whose car stalled on the expressway was not as interested in knowing that the tow truck driver's name was Bill Smith as they were in knowing that he was a mechanic! They were delighted to meet Bill Smith, the mechanic.

The daughter with the sick mother wasn't especially eager to meet James Wilson—until she knew he was James Wilson, the doctor.

And the frightened young woman who heard a prowler outside her apartment really didn't want to be introduced to Fred Martin and John Jones—until she saw that they were policemen.

The people in these examples are not particularly callous and unfeeling—all of us react in about the same way. When a pipe breaks under the sink and starts flooding the kitchen, we're far more interested in knowing that a man is a plumber and knows how to shut off the water than we are in being formally introduced to Charles Johnson, or whatever his name may be.

The names of God

The Hebrew word most often translated into English simply as "God" is *Elohim* (sometimes *El* or *Elah*). This name comes from words which mean strength, or the strong one, and to swear or bind oneself by an oath, implying faithfulness. So *El* or *Elohim*, used some 2,500 times in the Old Testament, emphasizes that God is the strong, faithful One. Facing a world of overwhelming forces and uncertain personal resources, man found himself in tremendous need of the strength and faithfulness of *Elohim*.

The second primary name of God, translated as Lord in English, is *Jehovah*, or the self-existent One. Literally, the word means, "He that is who He is, therefore the eternal I AM." But *Havah*, the Hebrew root from which *Jehovah* is formed, also signifies "to become," thus pointing to a continuous and increasing self-revelation. So *Jehovah* is the self-existent One who reveals Himself.

It is the name (*Havah*) that is used for God in Exodus 3:14 where Moses asks God what name he shall use to say who sent him to lead the Israelites out of Egypt. *And God said to Moses, I AM WHO I AM and WHAT I AM, and I WILL BE WHAT I WILL BE; and He said, You shall say this to the Israelites, I AM has sent me to you!* (Amplified Bible).

The third primary Hebrew word for God is *Adon* or *Adonai*, meaning Master. It is also translated into English as Lord. This name form suggests the worthiness of God to be obeyed and implies that He will provide direction and guidance in that service.

These primary Hebrew names for Deity were often combined with other words to help expand and enlarge man's understanding of God. There are

"I Am El Shaddai"

numerous compound uses of even the primary names, such as *Jehovah Elohim* and *Adonai Jehovah*, both translated Lord God.

But combined with other descriptive terms, the names of God open our understanding enough for us to catch a glimpse of His majesty and power. *El Olam* tells us that God is both everlasting and ruler over everlasting things. *El Elyon*, the highest or the most high God, is the possessor of both heaven and earth, and has unquestioned authority in both spheres. And *Jehovah Sabaoth* is Lord of Hosts, the God of unlimited power.

Perhaps some of the most beautiful and enlightening compound names of God are the various *Jehovah-* forms. When Abraham was about to sacrifice his son, Isaac, in obedience to God's command, the Lord stopped him from hurting the boy and supplied a ram to use as a substitute offering. In that experience, Abraham discovered that God was *Jehovah-jireh*, the Lord who provides.

He is also:

Jehovah-rapha, the Lord who heals;

Jehovah-nissi, the Lord our banner, symbol of victory in battle;

Jehovah-shalom, the Lord our peace;

Jehovah-ra-ah, the Lord my shepherd;

Jehovah-tsidkenu, the Lord our righteousness;

Jehovah-shammah, the Lord is present, which speaks of the abiding presence of God.

It is vitally important for you to understand that these different names do not signify different Gods, but different attributes or characteristics of the one, true God. Think of it in this way—suppose we were talking about a human individual named Joe Brown. You would have no trouble accepting Joe Brown as the son of Joseph Brown, the brother of Sue Brown, the husband of Marie Brown, and the father of Billy and Susie Brown, You would understand how he could be Joe Brown, the carpenter, the checker player, the little league coach, the owner of a blue Chevrolet, and a deacon at church. Joe Brown is who and what he needs to be to each person and in each function of his life.

And so is God—to an extent that far surpasses any example the human mind can devise.

Of all the names of God, the most touching and meaningful to me is *El Shaddai*. That name first appears in our Bible in Genesis 17, when God appeared to Abram and said, "*I am Almighty God*" (Verse 1). Again, the English translation fails to capture the depth and scope of the real meaning of the term.

We've already seen that *El* signifies the "Strong One." But the qualifying word, *Shaddai*, is what so impresses me. It is from the Hebrew word, *shad*, which means the breast. In fact, much of the time in the Old Testament it refers literally to a woman's breast. So *Shaddai* means primarily "the breasted."

What is the significance of this? God, as *Shaddai*, is the Nourisher, the Strength-giver, and thus, the Satisfier, who pours Himself into believing lives.

A mother who nurses her baby gives it strength and nourishment. And so much more! Her milk provides an immunity to disease. And the act of nursing promotes a bonding between mother and child. The infant, fretful and restless, is quieted, rested, and satisfied at its mother's breast. He is warm and secure in loving arms. He is comforted and soothed by hearing the familiar rhythm of his mother's heartbeat. He needs no other resource, no other fellowship than he receives at the breast. What he has is more than enough for his every need. God is our Strength, our Nourisher, and our Satisfier. In His presence—at His Breast—we receive immunity against all hurtful forces that might attack, and are comforted by the rhythm of the heart of God.

No other name of God—no other description captures the tenderness and all-sufficiency of our relationship to the Lord which is expressed by *El Shaddai*.

El Shaddai makes fruitful

But a study of the characteristic uses of the name in the Word of God reveals that *El Shaddai* not only enriches, but also makes fruitful. The Lord said to Abram, "I am Almighty God—*El Shaddai*—I will multiply you exceedingly ... I will make you exceedingly fruitful" (see Genesis 17:1, 2, 6).

Isn't that a beautiful promise? But do you realize to whom it was given? Yes, to Abram, who as a result of that divine promise changed his name from Abram (high father) to Abraham (father of many nations). But this man was 99 years old, and according to Hebrews 11:12, *as good as dead.*

He doesn't seem a likely prospect to become the father of many nations, does he, especially when his wife, who is past 90, has been barren all of her life. But *El Shaddai* says that the descendants of Abraham will be like the stars of the heavens and the sands of the sea—so numerous they are impossible to even count. And He asks Sarah, whose faith is small, *"Is anything too hard for the Lord?"* (Genesis 18:14).

I'm sure you know the story of how Isaac was born to Abraham and Sarah. From Isaac came Esau and Jacob, later known as Israel. And to Jacob were born 12 sons, each of whom became head of one of the tribes of Israel.

But that's not all! Abraham had also fathered a child by Sarah's Egyptian maid, Hagar. This son, Ishmael, also had 12 sons, who became tribal fathers and forefathers of the Arab people of today.

After the death of Sarah—more than 35 years after the birth of Isaac—Abraham took another wife, Keturah, who bore him six more sons! Finally, at the age of 175, Abraham died. He lived to see God's promise fulfilled. He had, indeed, been made fruitful. His descendants were so numerous they could no longer be counted. He had become the father of many nations.

El Shaddai our Purifier

El Shaddai is our Nourisher, our Strength-giver and Satisfier. He also makes us fruitful, multiplying us exceedingly. But once we become productive, He does not lose interest in us. Instead, *El Shaddai* becomes a chastening, purifying force to make us even more fruitful.

The story of Job is a classic example. Bible scholars say the Book of Job is probably the oldest of the Bible books—oldest not in the history it covers, but in terms of the date when it was written.

And interestingly enough, the characteristic name of God in Job, occurring 31 times, is *El Shaddai*, the Almighty.

"I Am El Shaddai"

The first thing we are told about Job is that he was a good man, who lived an exemplary life pleasing to God. He was the best man of his time. Job was prosperous, with a beautiful family and great possessions.

Then, through a vicious satanic attack, Job lost everything—his children, his sheep, oxen, donkeys, camels, and many of his servants. He was wiped out—ruined!

Job was hurt, grief-stricken, heartbroken. But do you know what he did? In the midst of his pain and loss, he worshipped God (see Job 1:20). "The Lord gave, and the Lord has taken away," he said. "Blessed be the name of the Lord" (see Verse 21).

Now we know Job was mistaken in saying that God had taken everything from him. His statement shows the inaccuracy of his understanding of the loving nature of a giving God. His statement was wrong, but his praise was right.

Keep in mind that Job had only a limited revelation of God—he lived before there were any written scriptures of the recorded experiences of others to pattern his life after. He could only see the unfoldment of God's nature and will toward him as he faced the unyielding challenges of the laboratory of life.

Although his understanding of God wasn't perfect and his statements were sometimes inaccurate, Job did know he could—and must—trust the Lord. So even in the midst of his sorrow, he praised God.

But the devil wasn't through! He sought permission to test Job further by afflicting his body ... and God allowed it. But notice this very carefully—God did not strike Job or make him sick, Satan did. The Bible says explicitly, *Then*

Satan went out ... and struck Job with painful boils from the sole of his foot to the crown of his head (2:7).

So terrible was Job's suffering that his wife couldn't bear to see him in such a state. "If God has done this to you, why don't you curse Him, die, and get out of your misery," she said.

Job's "friends" came around to speculate as to the cause of his misfortune. Was he being punished for some sin? Was he being disciplined to keep him from future disobedience? Job rejected their accusations, but did not sin against God, either by word or thought.

Job could have allowed all the religious ideas of man he heard to destroy his faith and turn Him against God. His "friends" certainly didn't hesitate to express their mistaken opinions. And Job listened to them all.

Perhaps he would have been better off not to have heard all their gloomy judgmental statements. His experience certainly can help us learn the importance of being selective about whom we associate with, the things we see and hear. That doesn't mean we aren't to go out in love to the world or not care about people. But having a close association with people who are constantly negative, foul-mouthed, or malicious in their spirit can pull us down to destruction. At times we need to shut ourselves away from outside influences and let God's presence pour through our inner being until we are running over with the positive power of His divine nature. Then we can go and influence others positively and for good instead of being contaminated by their negativism.

Make no mistake about it—Job did not like what had happened to him. Even worse, he did not understand why he was suffering. He was barely able to see that his own fear had opened him up and made him vulnerable to Satan's attack—*For the thing I greatly feared has come upon me, and what I dreaded has happened to me* (3:25).

But he decided to trust God, no matter what happened. He said, *Though He slay me, yet will I trust Him* (13:15). Again, his understanding of God was limited and mistaken to think that God would afflict or kill him. But his trust in God was faultless.

As he stepped out in faith, even in the middle of his ordeal, Job came to a wonderful realization about God. "*He knows every detail of what is happening to me; and when he has examined me, he will pronounce me ... as pure as solid gold*" (23:10, Living Bible).

No one escapes the trauma and problems of life. And within each of us, the ongoing drama of the Job-Satan conflict continues. Job represents the God-seeking part of us that almost instinctively reaches out to the renewing, sustaining, life-giving power of our Father-Creator. Satan represents that part of our nature or personality that is negative and failure-oriented. Triggered by fear, we try to blame ourselves for every disappointing event or circumstance, and allow our sense of unworthiness to depreciate every accomplishment or success.

Finally, Job comes face to face with a full revelation of the greatness of God ... and all his questions and uncertainties are resolved in the light and perspective of the majesty of the Lord. In an eloquent four-chapter discourse, God responds to Job's request for an explanation of his sufferings. He does not attempt to justify what has happened. He does not miraculously change the circumstances Job finds so grievous. Instead, He presents Himself—He reveals

His unlimited wisdom and power. Job discovers that the certainty of his faith is not linked to outward circumstances, nor to speculative human interpretations, but in the encounter of faith in an all-wise and all-powerful God.

And God the Almighty—*El Shaddai*—brought him through. Job wasn't spared the problems. He wasn't spared the trouble. He wasn't spared the heartache. He wasn't spared the suffering and pain.

But God brought him through it all … stronger, wiser, more compassionate and more productive than he had been before.

In fact, God sent Job's three false comforters to him to be prayed for. God said to Eliphaz, one of the "friends" who had accused Job of being sinful, "*My wrath is aroused against you and your two friends, for you have not spoken of Me what is right, as My servant Job has. Now therefore … go to my servant Job … and My servant Job shall pray for you. For I will accept him*" (42:7, 8).

Here's the beautiful part—God expanded Job's ministry! He used him to save someone else! He made him more productive than he had been before—a greater instrument for the kingdom of God. Job prayed for his friends that they would be restored to full fellowship with God, and that they would be blessed.

Did you know that what you make happen for others, God will make happen for you? That's part of God's law. Look what happened for Job when he prayed for his friends. *And the Lord restored Job's losses when he prayed for his friends. Indeed the Lord gave Job twice as much as he had before … Now the Lord blessed the latter days of Job more than his beginning* (42:10, 12).

"I Am El Shaddai"

My personal test of faith

I know how to relate to Job. In 1982, I went through a series of experiences that rocked me to the very core of my being. I suffered losses I thought I couldn't stand. I had sung and taught and preached about *El Shaddai*, the God of more than enough, in meetings across the nation. For several months I was given the opportunity to prove in my own life what I had so enthusiastically proclaimed. I had to demonstrate that My God was all sufficient, that He was the Almighty, that He could and would provide my every need.

My ordeal began with the sudden and totally unexpected death of my 25-year-old nephew, Greg Smith. He died at the beginning of his dreams, just as his ministry was getting started. He was as dear to me as a son. He had worked at my side in my ministry before launching out on his own. I felt that Greg had more potential than any young minister I'd ever known—I knew he would become a dynamic powerhouse for God. So great was my confidence that, unknown to him or anyone else, I wrote in my will that at my death all the assets of my own ministry were to go to a special missionary organization I had set up for him.

His death shook me, hurt me, almost crushed me. Even after I got over the shock and was able to accept his passing, at times the sense of loss would sweep over me in waves until my insides trembled so violently that I felt stabbing, physical pain.

But I came to some important understandings during this time of loss and grief. I came to realize that I was not to blame God for Greg's death ... nor was I to give the devil credit for destroying him. Greg was not a pawn in the hands of opposing supernatural forces—he just died.

However, God did use his death and the intense emotional sensitivity I experienced as a result to get my attention. This opened me up to hear something that, in the natural, seemed too illogical to consider. But this revolutionary set of instructions has proved itself to be a true revelation of the abundant *El Shaddai*.

A week after Greg's death, the Lord spoke to me in a dramatic and unmistakable way. Some time before, my brother and his family, Mother and I had all planned to meet in Tulsa to attend the reunion of Rhema Bible Training School graduates.

So after Greg's death, we went from my home in Dallas to Tulsa. I was in the Williams Plaza Hotel on the morning of April 8. 1982. I was not praying, but as is my habit, I was listening—meditating, staying open before the Lord.

Then, at 10:30 a.m.—I remember it exactly—God spoke to me and said, "Sell your home and your office building. Move your ministry to Tulsa and begin a one-hour daily television program to go into New England."

Then I had a vision—not a supernatural vision—but a clear vision through my spiritual eyes. I saw the hammer of the Spirit of God pounding away at the walls surrounding New England, breaking down the barriers. I could see that the one-hour-a-day program was needed to change the mentality of the people and help them recognize the healing love of God.

Following that vision, I went into the next room and told Mother what God had spoken to me. As always, she was in agreement with me. She simply said, "If that's what you believe, then go do it."

Two hours later we met my brother and his wife for lunch. Sitting at the table in the middle of the Taco Bueno on Memorial Drive, we had an impromptu board meeting and unanimously decided to do exactly what God had told me to do.

I knew if I didn't act on these decisions immediately that compromise would be too simple and easy. To the onlooker, my actions might have seemed impetuous, but that wasn't the case. I had been seeking God for direction about a television ministry for at least a year. His answer came to me in an instant. The things God asked me to do almost seemed more than I could handle at first. Then I could see that the greatness, the magnitude of God's revelation to me demanded instantaneous obedience or I would be tempted to water it down.

At first I didn't tell anyone what I was getting ready to do. I wasn't ready to try and explain it to anyone else. I knew it would be hard for them to understand. I mean, it didn't make any sense to give up my established life ... to abandon everything I had worked so hard for.

Then, there was the matter of finding new office space, a new staff, and a new place to live in Tulsa—a city I didn't especially like in the first place. And while I had been a guest on many TV programs, and had even produced my own ministry series under the sponsorship of a Christian network, what did I know about creating and producing a one-hour, daily TV program with an entirely new format? And with no crew, no equipment, no studio ... and limited money!

Several days later I finally told my friends what God was saying. A few of them caught the vision immediately. But sure enough, some friends thought the strain of Greg's death had caused me to overreact in a very dramatic and unrealistic way. Because it seemed so totally illogical.

But God's plan began to unfold—step by step—in ways nobody could ever have expected. I only know that almost overnight I had a buyer for my house. And the money I needed to move came in—at the last minute—from totally unexpected sources.

One day I stood, almost numb, and realized that I was leaving everything in the world that was dear to me. My house—my home—was gone and all my possessions were packed in cardboard boxes. I was leaving my friends and family—only Mother planned to move to Tulsa with me.

I understood a little of what Job must have felt. Losing family, possessions, fellow workers, friends—I was giving it all up.

But *El Shaddai* was at work in my behalf, even though I couldn't see Him at the moment. Almost before I knew what was going on, some of my closest friends in Dallas decided to come to Tulsa with me! These were more than just acquaintances—they were great people of prayer, fellow believers, people of like precious faith. Then God led me to what I can only describe as a dream house. It was so much nicer than my home in Dallas that it seemed unbelievable.

Getting the house was truly a miracle in itself. God had impressed me to give the profit from the sale of my home in Dallas to the ministry. So I gave away what would have been the down payment. When I gave those funds, I thought I would have to give up getting the new house—and I was willing to do it.

But the realtor who had shown me the lovely home in Tulsa wouldn't give up. She believed I was supposed to have that house, so she kept figuring and re-figuring financial arrangements that the bank and the owner might accept.

Finally—even as the movers were loading up my furniture and possessions in Dallas—she got a deal worked out that everybody was willing to accept. But it still required more down payment money than I had … I thought. Suddenly I remembered two life insurance policies I'd had for several years. I found they had enough cash value to pay the bank. And the house God provided was ready … just when I needed it.

After looking at several potential locations, I still hadn't found suitable office space … and time was running out. So I went to see Daisy Osborn and told her what God was doing in my life and ministry, and explained my need for office space. "Is there any place at all you have available, or could refer me to?" I asked.

Daisy and her husband, Rev. T.L. Osborn, didn't know me well. But they were so loving and gracious to me. They asked their daughter and son-in-law to move out of a large apartment in the Osborn Foundation building to make a place for us. It was an ideal office location, with space that was functional and reasonable.

At times I almost had to pinch myself to see if I was dreaming. I could hardly believe what I saw taking place before my very eyes.

But the challenges to my faith were far from over. There was still the matter of a one-hour, daily TV program. Before I was sure of any of the details, I called on many pastors and Christian leaders in the Tulsa area and confidently assured them that I would be on the air soon, that God had told me to launch a new television ministry.

The story of how it all came to pass would fill a book. Every day brought a new opportunity to take another step of faith. New stations were added to our network, and the programs had an impact—particularly in the New England area—that is almost unbelievable. We saw a tremendous revival on the eastern seaboard.

But the most gratifying thing of all is that my own ministry vision had quadrupled ... then quadrupled again. I was convinced we had only scratched the surface of what God was going to help us to accomplish for Him.

Everything I "gave up" for the Lord has come back to me multiplied many times over. Every sacrifice has proved to be the seed of ever-increasing blessings. And in every challenge—in every situation for which I could see no answer or solution—*El Shaddai* has proven that He is my Supplier, the God of more than enough.

If God can bless me, He'll bless you.

If He will meet my need, He'll meet yours. If *El Shaddai* is more than enough in my life, He'll be more than enough in yours.

God will not fail you. He will always meet you at the point of your need. He asks only for your obedience, your faith, your commitment to Him.

What do you have to give to God? *Give it!*

What is it you can do for God? *Do it!*

What do you need from God? *Expect it!*

Your God is *El Shaddai*—nothing is impossible.

Now pray with me—

EL SHADDAI, my powerful Father God, how I love You. All of my life I have longed to know You … to touch You. Always I have sensed You, yet I am only now aware of Your consuming care. Beloved Father, my strength-giver, thank You for all You are, and for the fact that all is mine in Christ. Lord, I commit myself into Your keeping power, Your loving concern. I give all to You—the problems, trials, and cares of life that have burdened me are now in Your miracle-working hands. I rest in You because You are now working on my behalf, solving my problems. Thank You for being the God of the impossible.

chapter
two

more than enough for your salvation

ONE OF THE THINGS I love most about the ministry God has given me is the opportunity to meet so many interesting people. I often wish I could spend more time getting better acquainted with the people who attend my services and watch my television programs.

I have discovered that many of these friends are having real problems in the area of their personal salvation. Sometimes I meet an individual—or get a letter from a person—who says, "Vicki, I know I need to be saved. The salvation experience you talk about sounds so wonderful. But you just don't know how bad I have been—how terrible my life is. I'm afraid I've fallen too low and made too big a mess of things for God to even want me."

What a thrill to tell such a person that God is able to save to the uttermost—that His grace is sufficient for any and all sin. I try to help him or her realize that all sin is the same in God's eyes—that *all have sinned and fall short of the glory of God* (Romans 3:23). Once a person accepts this truth, he is willing to turn loose of all his anxiety and the crushing load of sin and be made a new creature.

There is such joy in knowing that God is able to take away all sin—that He is more than enough for our salvation. Unfortunately, some people fail to understand that when God forgives our sin, He forgets it as well. The Lord says, *"For I will forgive their iniquity, and their sin I will remember no more"* (Jeremiah 31:34).

Once confessed and forgiven, we are to forget our past sin and go on to new strength through the power of God. Paul, the great apostle, said, *One thing I do, forgetting those things which are behind and reaching forward to those things which are ahead, I press toward the goal for the prize of the upward call of God in Christ Jesus. Therefore let us, as many as are mature, have this mind* (Philippians 3:13-15).

My heart goes out to the poor, frightened people who come to me and say, "Vicki, pray that I'll have the assurance that I'm right with God—that I'm saved." I say to them, "God is more than enough for your salvation. When you confessed your sin and asked Him to come into your life, He did. And once He did, that settled it forever … unless you willfully renounce Him."

Often I talk with people who have tried to live for God for many years, but have never had the joy of salvation and the assurance of God's continuing mercy working in their life. "But you see, I'm afraid I may have missed God's will and failed," they say.

Do you know what my answer is? "Join the rest of us!" Missing God's will temporarily is not a terminal condition. God's love is constant—His leading is always available. When we stumble, or stray away, the Holy Spirit never stops working to remind us of Jesus and draw us back into perfect fellowship with

more than enough for your salvation

Him. Oh, I love what the prophet Jeremiah wrote—*Through the Lord's mercies we are not consumed, because His compassions fail not. They are new every morning; Great is Your faithfulness* (Lamentations 3:22, 23).

The fifteenth chapter of Luke contains some of the most powerful teaching about salvation to be found in the entire Bible. In this section of Scripture, Jesus relates three parables about being lost … and found.

First, He tells about a man with 100 sheep. If one wanders away, he leaves the 99 in a safe place and goes to search for the lost sheep. Finding it, he puts it on his shoulder and tenderly carries it back home. Then he calls his friends to rejoice with him because the lost is found.

The second parable is about a woman who loses one of her 10 silver coins. She lights a lamp, sweeps the floor, and searches diligently until she finds the coin. Then she calls all her neighbors to celebrate with her because she has found what was lost.

And the third parable is the most moving of all—the story of the prodigal son. You know the story—a young man asks for his inheritance and deliberately goes away from his family. In a far country, he squanders all he was given, and ends up in a pigpen, slopping the hogs. In that wretched state, he comes to himself and decides to go home—to ask to be just a servant in his father's house. And he started back home. While he was still a long way off, his father saw him and ran to meet him, welcoming him back home. He was restored to full fellowship in the family, with clean clothes, a gold ring, new shoes, and a joyful feast with his neighbors and friends.

These powerful parables are important on two levels. First, they help us understand that God wants us to be found no matter how we became lost. Like the coin that fell off the woman's table and rolled into a dark corner—we may have been lost—victims of circumstance—because we didn't know we could be saved. We may have grown up in a home that never mentioned the name of Jesus or taught the truth of God's Word.

Perhaps we got lost because of our own ignorance or carelessness, like the sheep that wandered away. It didn't intend to get lost—it just wandered a while and then couldn't find its way back. Your life may have been like a lost sheep.

Or, you may have been like the prodigal son to some extent. You got lost on purpose. You went away from God deliberately, determined to do your own thing and live your own life. It may have taken some time before you discovered that you had wasted what had been given to you, and you decided to come back to the Father and ask to just be a servant in His house.

No matter which situation describes your experience, one thing is the same. There was a desire on God's part for you to be "found"—to be saved and restored. And when you did accept salvation, there was great joy and thanksgiving by the friends of God.

Secondly, I believe these three parables also relate to each of us in our inner being—this is the second level of understanding. The coin refers to that part of us that is incomplete … that one part of our life that isn't perfected and so is, in a sense, lost. The sheep refers to the "crazy" part of our personality, that aspect of our being that wanders off willy-nilly in no direction. It's that one part of us we just can't seem to get under control. But God's salvation is more than enough for our "sheep nature"—He goes out and finds us and tenderly carries us back to the protection of His fold.

Each of us, of course, has a prodigal son part of our nature. This is the part that deliberately goes away from the Father at times—that seeks to get lost on purpose. And this part of us cannot and will not be saved until we want it to be. God will find the "coin" part of us … He will search and bring back the "sheep" part of us. But the "prodigal son" part of our inner being is entirely in our control. We can stay in the far country away from God, or we can choose to move back toward our Father. He will not bother us or force His attention on us as long as we deliberately stay away. But when we come to ourself and say, "I'll go back to my Father," while we are still a long way off, He comes to meet us, to wrap us in His loving arms and welcome us back into full fellowship with the family. And He restores what we have lost and wasted. He gives it back to us and gives us a new opportunity.

Isn't that beautiful? That's how all-sufficient God's salvation is. It reaches us on all levels. And it helps us see that God wants to save us even more than we desire to be saved. If we come to Him, He will not refuse us or cast us away. How great and how wonderful is the love and grace of Christ our Redeemer!

Now, let me share with you some more promises from God's Word that will help you see just how great your salvation really is. You need never be tormented by doubt and guilt again. You have the absolute assurance that your sin is forgiven and forgotten and that you are eternally God's child.

No longer do you have to struggle with guilt and condemnation. In fact, God doesn't want you to. John 3:17 says, *"For God did not send His Son into the world to condemn the world, but that the world through Him might be saved."* El Shaddai—the God of more than enough, wants to deliver you from all guilt and condemnation. Why? Because guilt invariably produces fear. A guilty person is always afraid of being discovered and punished. Fear is a terrible thing. It does awful things to people—to their spirits and their bodies. But one of the most destructive aspects of fear is negative thinking. Faith cannot coexist with negative thinking. And God's Word declares that *without faith it is impossible to please Him* (Hebrews 11:6).

How can you come to God and ask for His help if you're afraid He is going to punish you? You can't. You can only come to love God and trust Him when you believe He does not want to condemn you for your sin but set you free.

As I said before, I have counseled with people who had done some pretty horrible things in their lives. They felt such overwhelming guilt about what they'd done that they couldn't believe God would forgive them. But He did—as soon as they accepted that He was willing and eager to help them become new creatures, to die to their old life and be born again.

Their *El Shaddai* revealed Himself to them as the God of more than enough for their wholeness, their salvation! The Greek words translated *salvation* actually speak of health, deliverance, safety, and victory. In their fullest meaning, they express the idea that to receive salvation means to be rescued and defended.

If you feel guilty and condemned, let me assure you that the God of more than enough is able—and ready—to forgive you of *all* your sin right now. Jesus said, *"The one who comes to Me I will by no means cast out"* (John 6:37). James 4:8 says, *"Draw near to God and He will draw near to you."*

It doesn't matter what you've done or haven't done. It doesn't matter how many times you've failed. God has more than enough love, mercy, and forgiveness to cleanse every mistake and give you a brand-new lease on life. As far as the east is from the west, that's how far He will remove your sin from you (see Psalms 103:12).

And with the sin, He removes the guilt and condemnation. *There is therefore now no condemnation to those who are in Christ Jesus, who do not walk according to the flesh, but according to the Spirit. For the law of the Spirit of life in Christ Jesus has made me free from the law of sin and death* (Romans 8:1, 2).

How do you go about getting God's forgiveness? His only requirements are that you repent, believe on Jesus as your Lord and Saviour, and publicly confess Him before men. On the day of Pentecost, Peter stood up and preached to the multitude that had gathered. He told them to, *Repent—change your views, and purpose to accept the will of God in your inner selves instead of rejecting it—and be baptized every one of you in the name of Jesus Christ for the forgiveness of and release from your sins* (Acts 2:38, Amplified).

Notice that to repent means more than just saying, "I'm sorry." True repentance means "changing your views, to think differently." Actually, in the original language, repent had an even stronger meaning—"to turn around and go the opposite direction … to turn to a better way of life."

The apostle Paul, testifying to King Agrippa, defined repentance in definite, explicit terms. He said men *should repent and turn to God and do works and live lives consistent with and worthy of their repentance* (Acts 26:20, Amplified).

> *If you confess with your mouth the Lord Jesus and believe in your heart that God has raised Him from the dead, you will be saved. For with the heart one believes to righteousness, and with the mouth confession is made to salvation* (Romans 10:9, 10).

When that happens, you become a brand-new creation! *Therefore, if anyone is in Christ, he is a new creation; old things have passed away; behold, all things have become new ... For He made Him who knew no sin to be sin for us, that we might become the righteousness of God in Him* (2 Corinthians 5:17, 21).

You don't have to feel guilty and condemned anymore, because you are a brand-new creature. It is as if you had never sinned. God wipes your record clean and gives you a new start.

And that is only the beginning. When you accept Christ, He comes and dwells within you. The God of more than enough takes up residence in your heart. He fills you with the strength and power of His Holy Spirit. Jesus once walked on this earth in a physical body, but now He walks on the earth in you. You are His hands and feet, reaching out in love to help the needy.

When Jesus sent out His 12 disciples, He said, *"Do not worry about how or what you should speak. For it will be given to you in that hour what you should speak; for it is not you who speaks, but the Spirit of your Father who speaks in you"* (Matthew 10:19, 20).

God originally planned for His relationship with man to be a warm, intimate, personal friendship. He wanted to walk with man and talk with him. He wanted to abide with man and have fellowship with him. But sin changed all that.

When God made Adam, they had perfect fellowship. And God gave Adam dominion over all things. Adam was like God. He was made in His image. However, Adam's sinful disobedience forfeited his perfect relationship to God and his dominion over all creation. Through Adam's sin, mankind was separated from full fellowship with God. Over the centuries, God has spoken to man through His prophets, but satan's influence prevailed. Covenants were broken, promises went unkept. Man continually failed to keep his end of every bargain struck with God through his ignorance—by not **fully understanding the true nature of God.**

Only a remnant remained true. Many of them are listed in God's "Hall of Fame" in Hebrews 11. Verse 13 describes these heroes of faith: *These all died in faith, not having received the promises, but having seen them afar off were assured of them, embraced them, and confessed that they were strangers and pilgrims on the earth.*

Then Jesus came and once and for all redeemed man from satan's domination. And when you accept His redemption, God restores His relationship with you and gives you dominion over all things.

The God of more than enough gives you new hope, new life, new power. He elevates you to your proper position. He comes and dwells in you. And He even goes further and makes you *His child.*

> *But as many as received Him, to them He gave the right to become children of God, even to those who believe in His name* (John 1:12).

Can you comprehend that? The God of the universe, Maker of heaven and earth, chooses to make YOU His child. He adopts you into His royal family and gives you all the rights, privileges, and riches you are entitled to as an heir of God.

> *For as many as are led by the Spirit of God, these are sons of God. For you did not receive the spirit of bondage again to fear, but you received the Spirit of adoption by whom we cry out, "Abba, Father." The Spirit Himself bears witness with our spirit that*

we are children of God, and if children, then heirs—heirs of God and joint heirs with Christ (Romans 8:14-17).

You are an heir of God, and a joint heir with Jesus Christ. All that God has is yours—not only in the world to come, but now … in this day and hour.

What exactly are those riches? In the following chapters we'll see exactly how you can claim all God has promised you for every area of your life. But here are a few of the things you've inherited.

Jesus said, *"Most assuredly, I say to you, he who believes in Me, the works that I do he will do also; and greater works than these he will do, because I go to My Father. And whatever you ask in My name, that I will do, that the Father may be glorified in the Son. If you ask anything in My name, I will do it"* (John 14:12-14).

With Christ living in you, you can do all things (see Philippians 4:13). You'll even do greater things than Jesus did while He was here on earth.

How will you be able to do these things? Through the power of God. Acts 1:8 promises, *"You shall receive power when the Holy Spirit has come upon you."* And you are included in Acts 2:39, *"For the promise is to you and to your children, and to all who are afar off, as many as the Lord our God will call."*

No matter what the circumstance or situation might be that you face today, you have God's promise that He will help you triumph over it by making it turn out for your good. *We know that all things work together for good to those who love God, to those who are the called according to his purpose* (Romans 8:28).

In fact, God promises that because you are His child, you are going to reign not only in the life to come, but in this life. *For if by the one man's offense death reigned through the one, much more those who receive abundance of grace and of the gift of righteousness WILL REIGN IN LIFE through the One, Jesus Christ* (Romans 5:17).

You are to *reign in life!* You are to prosper ... enjoy good health ... have peace of mind ... build a happy home ... work miracles. You are a partaker of God's divine nature.

El Shaddai, the God of more than enough promises you all these things—and more—when you give your life to Him. He is more than enough for your salvation ... more than enough to cleanse every sin and set you free from guilt and fear.

But none of these truths apply until you are born into the family of God and have the assurance of your position in Him. But that can happen for you in this moment—in an instant of time.

May it happen even now as we pray together!

For your personal salvation—

Father, I come to You to tell You I believe Jesus is Your Son who died for me that I might have eternal life. I believe He was raised from the dead and lives now. Come into my heart, Lord Jesus. Now I know I am a new creature in Christ Jesus and old things have passed away. Satan has no power over me and I am free from all bondage. My mind is now the mind of Christ and I confess His healing in the areas of my life that are marred by sin. No longer am I a slave to habits—Jesus is setting me free. Thank you, Father, for my salvation. In Jesus' Name, Amen.

For your family and friends who need to know Christ …

My dear Father God, I lift _____ to You now because Mark 11:24 tells me to believe I receive when I pray. Therefore, I break the power of Satan over _____ and ask You to send laborers to cross their path and lead them into salvation. You have said in Your Word that we and our household should be saved. I confess it, placing my trust in Your living Word. Now, I praise You for their new life in Christ. Amen.

chapter three

more than enough for your inner power

I LOVE TO READ THE history of creation in Genesis—the Bible account of how God created the heavens and the earth, and all that is in the earth.

Have you ever noticed that five times during the creation God looked at what He had brought into being and saw that is was good? That's right! As each part of the universe began to function, and as the plants, animals, and sea creatures took their place, God approved what He had done. The Bible says, *And God saw that it was good* (Genesis 1:10, 12, 18, 21, 25). Then came the creation of mankind. *God said, "Let us make man in Our image, according to Our likeness"* (Verse 26). So God made man and gave him dominion—that is, sovereign authority, the right of absolute possession and use—over everything in the earth.

Now God looked again at all He had created, including the man and woman He had placed in authority there. But this time it was different! With the addition of mankind, His highest creation, made in His own image, God looked at what He had made, *and indeed it was very good* (Verse 31).

Do you see it? Can you grasp what God's opinion of you and me is? When He looked at the wonders of the universe—the planets, stars, the sun and moon … when He looked at all the grasses, herbs, plants, and trees … when He looked at all the fish, birds, and animals—God saw that it was good. But when He made man in His own image and gave him dominion over all the creation, God saw that indeed it *was very good!*

Why was man so important? What made him so distinctive, so different from all the rest of creation? Because man was made in the image and likeness of God! Because God breathed into his nostrils the breath of life—that unique divine force possessed by no other living creature. Man became a "living being"—within him was placed a God-likeness from the very fabric of eternity.

Genesis 2:7 says: *And the Lord God formed man of the dust of the ground, and breathed into his nostrils the breath of life; and man became a living being.*

Dr. Roy Blizzard, who for years was an instructor of biblical archeology, biblical history, and Hebrew at the University of Texas, paints a dramatic picture of man's creation in his translation of this verse. According to his studies of the ancient Hebrew texts, it actually reads: "And the Lord God Elohim created Adam from the minute particles of the totality of all that God is."

Isn't that a tremendous thought? The "dust" out of which we were formed was actually the minute particles of the reality of God! Not only are we made in the image and likeness of God, but the divine life force of the Creator is actually within us—an unlimited and unconquerable inner power.

more than enough for your inner power

The psalmist David wrote, *What is man, that You are mindful of him, and the son of [earthborn] man, that You care for him? Yet You have made him but little lower than God [or heavenly beings], and You have crowned him with glory and honor. You made him to have dominion over the works of Your hands; You have put all things under his feet* (Psalm 8:4-6, Amplified).

The psalmist goes on to describe the authority God has given man in Psalm 82:6: *I said, You are gods [since you judge on My behalf, as My representatives]; indeed, all of you are children of the Most High* (Amplified).

Wouldn't you think that God's highest creation, a being made in the image of God, would step out in confidence, head held high, standing tall and proud? Why would such an individual crawl through life on his hands and knees, defeated and fearful, cringing and shaking?

Yet I meet so many Christians who do not realize who they are—that they are shaped in God's likeness and filled with His power. They have not yet learned to draw upon the unlimited spiritual energy within them—the inner power flowing from *El Shaddai* that makes them more than conquerors in every situation they face.

The reason believers sometimes feel weak and helpless is that they focus on the outer world and respond to the wrong influences around them. They react with feelings ... and feelings can easily be manipulated by the enemy.

To be victorious—to win over earthly adversity or negative spiritual forces—we must bring our inner power to bear on the problem. How can we do this? By meditating ... concentrating on the very essence of God that makes up our most intimate inner being—that flow of sheer spiritual power that is activated within us through the Word of God.

Isaiah understood it when he declared, *But those who wait on the Lord shall renew their strength; they shall mount up with wings like eagles, they shall run and not be weary, they shall walk and not faint* (Isaiah 40:31).

You can do this. Center your thinking on the *El Shaddai* force within you. It helps if you learn to visualize … to see with the eyes of your spirit. When I "see" the power of *El Shaddai*, it is a force exploding out of my inner being, not something being poured in from the outside! I see Him within me all the time. The inner power is not contained in the "bucket" of my heart—a container that must constantly be refilled. The inner power is like an artesian spring that constantly bubbles and flows a stream of divine energy into my life.

Then, I visualize myself constantly in the presence of the Lord. I am never alone. I may be by myself, with no other people around, but God is always with me. He goes everywhere I go—I'm constantly aware that He is with me. He's with you, too, but you will not discover the reality of unending fellowship with Him until you consciously begin to visualize Him.

I heard of an old Chinese gentleman who became a Christian late in his life. So vivid was his personal experience with the Lord and so refreshingly simple was his faith that he treated the Lord as his constant companion. Each day when he woke up and started getting dressed, he would say happily, "Good morning, Lord. Where we go today, Jesus?"

Ah, that's the secret—*Christ in you, the hope of glory* (Colossians 1:27). That is the source of inner power *El Shaddai* causes to overflow from deep inside us. No wonder the beloved apostle wrote, *You are of God, little children, and have overcome … because He who is in you is greater than he who is in the world* (1 John 4:4).

more than enough for your inner power

Once you begin to see through eyes of faith just how tremendous your inner power source is, you can start accomplishing great things for God. The way to have effective faith ... the way to direct your inner power to productive work for the kingdom is to keep on visualizing.

When you want to achieve something, hold in your spirit a picture of yourself achieving it. Paint in all the details. Make it as real as you possibly can. The image you form and hold in your conscious mind will pass into the subconscious mind, gearing up every ounce of natural energy and ability you have to reach your goal. But more than that, visualizing also releases an unseen but all-powerful faith force that directs all the strength and resources of *El Shaddai*—the God of more than enough—to your assistance.

You may not see it ... but it's working.

You may not hear it ... but it's there.

You may not even understand what's happening ... but the full resources of Heaven are brought into play to accomplish what you set out to achieve.

You become what you believe ... what you visualize and allow your inner power to bring to pass. A high-jumper doesn't begin to run until he can visualize himself skimming over the bar. A golfer doesn't swing the club until he can "see" the ball soaring over the treetops and landing on the green.

Do you understand just how powerful you can be? Are you starting to realize the scope of what *El Shaddai* wants to help you accomplish? Dare to believe the impossible! Dare to dream and reach far beyond the limitations of human ability or resources. Dare to share the faith promise of *El Shaddai*, who *calls those things which do not exist as though they did* (Romans 4:17).

Consider the pyramids of Egypt, the Parthenon of Greece, the towering skyscrapers of America's cities, the massive "mind-power" of a complex computer system. What do they have in common? Each of them began as a germ of an idea that somebody visualized. Eventually each of those images took on form and substance and came bursting into triumphant reality.

Can you imagine—do you dare to consider—what you can accomplish with the added dimension of *El Shaddai's* spiritual resources flooding through your mind? It's absolutely awesome, isn't it?

Am I trying to say that your accomplishments ought to be automatic, effortless, routine? Not at all. Any significant achievement calls for great sacrifice and your best effort. But the difference between scaling the mountain or never starting to climb may well be knowing the inner power that is yours.

One of the hardest things God ever asked me to do was to begin our new daily television ministry. Just going back on TV was not the difficult thing, although I was well aware of what a massive undertaking it is to prepare and produce a one-hour program with taste, style, and solid content every single day. The hard part for me was accepting God's direction to move my entire ministry from Dallas, Texas to Tulsa, Oklahoma. That was hard because it meant leaving my established office and staff. It meant selling my house. It meant leaving a major metropolitan city and moving to a smaller city I had never particularly liked. It meant leaving all my acquaintances and close personal friends who lived in the Dallas area.

More than that, from a business and economic viewpoint, it seemed like the worst possible time to make such a move. High interest rates, for example, would seem to make finding a buyer for my house and a buyer for our office building difficult.

In the meantime, I had to make plans and start up a complete new ministry operation in Tulsa ... with limited resources. I had to find new office space. I had to find a new house. I had to hire and train a new staff. And I had to create an entirely new television format!

Besides planning what the new program was to be, there was the matter of finding a production facility, designing and building sets, finding a director, a crew, a staff of telephone prayer counselors, and taking care of literally hundreds of other details. We had to find air time in the areas God was directing us to reach, and believe for the enormous financial budget the new daily television ministry would require.

Does that sound effortless or automatic? Of course not! It was overwhelming. In the natural it was frightening ... absolutely mind-boggling.

Despite my own reluctance to pull up roots, move, and plunge into the new ministry, my soul was stirred. I felt an excitement that was almost uncontrollable at times. Right then I began to visualize what God had told me to do. I "saw" myself in a new home, a new office, and on the set of a TV studio producing a new, Spirit-anointed program. But more than that, I visualized the program being beamed into multiplied thousands of homes in the Midwest and New England areas. I saw people being healed as they watched the telecast. I saw people who would never darken the door of any church tune in our program and receive the good news of God's love.

Nothing had come to pass yet, you understand. I was just visualizing ... seeing with the eyes of faith ... speaking of future events with as much certainty as though they were already past. And I must admit that at times my vision got a bit hazy!

Especially when some well-meaning friends and comforters came to help me. "Vicki, you're missing God," they said. Oh, that helped so much because the old devil was trying to tell me that, too. And if I stopped to look at the whole situation logically, it didn't seem to make any sense to me either. But I knew what God was saying. And I knew I had to get away from the "help" of some of my friends.

Now I can look back and even be thankful for the concern and good intentions of the people who came to me. But it was hard to handle at the time. Yet it helped me to learn some important lessons.

First, I learned to watch who I talked to, or let talk to me, in order to protect the vision God had given me. I had to keep feeding my faith with the Word of God. I had to keep reminding myself that God didn't call everybody else to my vision—He called me. So, instead of listening to the opinions of others, I had to keep going back to God and living in the vision.

Second, I learned that I couldn't let man corrupt and dilute what God had told me to do. You see, my family and friends—the people closest to me—wanted to make things easier for me. "Oh, Vicki, I know you'll do all these wonderful things God is calling you to do, but you can only do so much at a time. Just don't move too fast and bite off more than you can chew. Take it a little slower and easier."

Do you see how insidious that kind of "encouragement" can be? I'm convinced that if I had surrounded myself with all who wanted to talk to me and

more than enough for your inner power

listened to what everybody had to say, I'd still be in Dallas ... miserable inside from knowing that I had missed God's best.

So I kept away from people ... spent lots of time alone. Now I'm not suggesting that we have to isolate ourselves from everybody. We need others for fellowship, and there is a time to go to them for counsel. But in times of growth, no one can stretch for you. Having someone else do your exercises doesn't get you in condition, and having them constantly caution you not to strain yourself and get your muscles all sore doesn't help much either. There are times you have to lock the door and get to work, stretching, straining, sweating ... until new strength comes surging into every muscle and cell.

One by one, a few at a time, God began to send some people of like precious faith to nurture me and support me. They knew that if I said God had told me to do it, God would bring it all to pass. And they joined me in intercessory prayer.

But even with their added support, there came the day when I had gone as far as I could go. Nothing was resolved ... nothing had fallen into place. And God was leading me to go to each of the leading pastors and Christian leaders in Tulsa and tell them that I was launching a new one-hour television ministry and was looking forward to serving them and having fellowship with them. I still had no evidence that what God had told me would come to pass, and I just didn't think I could go out on the limb even further and declare to my fellow ministers what was going to happen.

So I had a serious talk with the Lord. I said, "God, You've got to come forth. I've gone as far as I can go on faith alone. I can't go any further. I'm tired. I'm leaving everything I have, everything I know, everything I understand. I'm leaving all that's important to me and coming to a town I don't even want to come to. Now Lord, I have no evidence that what You've told me is happening. So far, all I've done is just talk. I must have confirmation from You within 24 hours.

Do you know what my inner circle of friends and I did next?

We had a party! That's right. We had the most beautiful party you've ever seen. We had the best china, the best silver, a lovely tablecloth, all the decorations, balloons, noisemakers—the works! We called it our "Count It All Joy" party.

You see, the apostle James said, *Count it all joy when you fall into various trials, knowing that the testing of your faith produces patience. But let patience have its perfect work, that you may be perfect and complete, lacking nothing* (James 1:2-4).

I'm told that James' directive to "count it all joy" is an idiom that actually means to throw or hurl a party. And that's exactly what we did. I've never felt less like having a party in my whole life. I almost choked on the food because I felt so much grief inside. I thought I was going to break into tears.

But I didn't. I ate the food. I laughed with my friends. We celebrated as if everything God had talked to me about had been fulfilled and was a reality. We kept on rejoicing and praising God until the awful burden, the crushing spirit of heaviness began to lift. I could actually sense myself getting stronger.

If I'd never understood it before, I knew exactly what the Word meant when it says, "*Do not sorrow, for the joy of the Lord is your strength*" (Nehemiah 8:10).

more than enough for your inner power

The very next day I was introduced to a couple who were intensely interested in my ministry. When they learned I was preparing to move from Dallas to Tulsa, they said, "Vicki, will you answer a question for us?" And I said I would.

"Could you use $1,000 to help you move?"

I didn't have a nickel! So I nodded and said, "Sure."

The lady sat down to write out a check, and suddenly the husband bent over and whispered something in her ear. Tears streamed down her face and she nodded yes. He looked up at me and said, "God says we are to make it $5,000."

It was my turn to cry! For unknown to them, that was the exact amount I needed to move. As I held that check in my hand, I realized that God was giving me the confirmation I had asked for ... within 24 hours.

And He wasn't through. Before that day was out, someone contacted my realtor in Dallas, and wanted to buy my house ... for cash. They didn't ask me to come down a penny on the price I was asking!

That was the beginning of the breakthrough. There were many obstacles left. However, this assurance from God caused my faith to grow at an accelerated rate.

From that day, I knew that everything God was leading me to do would come to pass. I knew that He would give me the strength and inner power to meet every challenge. And He did ... and He is still doing it today.

My experience is not unique. What God is doing in my life is available in your life too. Oh, your calling, your challenge may not be even remotely similar to mine. But the **inner power you need to carry out your calling** is just as available to you.

Through the limitless power of *El Shaddai*—the God of more than enough—you can be a tireless dynamo in God. When you tap into the power source of the universe, you receive the *energeia* of God. He becomes your "energizer" for life.

First, He gives you *exousia*, or divine authority. That's yours the moment you accept Jesus as your Lord and Saviour. He gives every child of God the "power of attorney" to conduct the Father's business.

That authority—when used with knowledge—renders Satan powerless. It's the "clout" that Jesus gave His disciples (that's you and me) in Luke 10:19: *"Behold, I give you the authority … over all the power of the enemy, and nothing shall by any means hurt you."*

That is the same authority He gave the 12 disciples in Luke 9:1: *Then He called His twelve disciples together and gave them power and authority over all demons, and to cure diseases.*

Second, when you step out to minister in the power of the Holy Spirit, He gives you *dunamis*, or miracle-working power. That's what Jesus promised in Acts 1:8: *"But you shall receive power when the Holy Spirit has come upon you."*

And it's the same power Jesus used in His ministry on earth. *"God anointed Jesus of Nazareth with the Holy Spirit and with power, who went about doing good and healing all who were oppressed by the devil, for God was with Him"* (Acts 10:38).

God was with Him … and He is with you. Any time Satan challenges your authority—and he will—you can back it up with supernatural power. Holy Spirit-filled believers carry a big stick!

more than enough for your inner power

And third, as you grow in faith you develop kratos—the kind of strength described in Ephesians 6:10: *Finally, my brethren, be strong in the Lord and in the power of His might.*

You walk with quiet *exousia*, or authority, with instant access to the adrenalin of *dunamis* power, shielded and protected by the *kratos* of God's might.

You're no longer just a reservoir of God's goodness. You are a conduit of His power. The immeasurable force of *El Shaddai* flows from your being!

You can move mountains. You can speak healing and deliverance to those you meet. You can lead men and women out of the darkness and into the light.

I challenge you to put *El Shaddai* to the test. Look your toughest problem right in the face, and then—with nothing wavering—say, "With God's help, I will defeat you. You cannot stand in the presence of Almighty God."

When you speak the Word of God—with no doubt or unbelief—miracles happen. You are going to discover a greater strength than you've ever known before. You'll never again be defeated. Even when the battle seems to be going to the enemy, you'll have the assurance that ultimate victory is yours.

There's no question about it. The Bible says, *Thanks be to God who ALWAYS leads us in triumph* (2 Corinthians 2:14). Unlimited power flows through you as a believer. But you have to turn on the switch. You have to be an open channel.

May the strength of *El Shaddai* gush forth from you today!

Let's pray—

God, my Lord, it seemed so hard to follow you. Now, I know You are inside—leading, guiding, and directing me into Your Divine Will. Forgive my unwillingness to stretch, to grow. Now that I realize You are my source, my power, my life, I am not afraid. You are my strength and provider. Lord, I open myself to Your perfect plan for my life and embrace all that You have for me. I know You lead me into pleasant places. Though the way there may seem dark and unsure, You guide me by Your precious Spirit. I am comforted in my heart with the assurance of Your loving concern for me. Forgive me for complaining—You have never caused a problem ... I have. Now I realize that You have been sending answers in many forms. How I treasure this new awakening. I will become aware of You and Your ways continually, my Father. I know that greater are You who is within me than he who is in the world. Amen.

My Father,
I treasure Your Word enough to meditate it, speak it, believe it and walk it — THAT You may be revealed to the World through me. Thank You for stirring me w/ confidence in who I am w/ You living inside me —
El Shaddai — I love You
Yours, Grace

chapter four

more than enough for your healing

GOOD HEALTH IS A GIFT of God.

El Shaddai—the God of more than enough—wants you to be healthy. He is your Source, not only for receiving healing, but also for walking in continued health.

Now a lot of people don't know that. They've been taught to believe that God is responsible for all human suffering—that when you get sick, God makes you sick. These people also believe that when you become a Christian, the poorer you are the more like Christ you are.

It's simply amazing that literally millions of people have a warped concept of God. They think of Him as some awesome, stern Being sitting on a throne in the heavens, who is upset with us and ready to punish us at the slightest misstep.

They don't understand that God is loving and good and has unlimited power available to heal their hurts and solve their problems. They don't know Christ can—and does—perform miracles today exactly as He did when He was on the earth 2,000 years ago.

They haven't heard about *El Shaddai*—the God of more than enough—who *is able to do exceedingly abundantly above all that we ask or think, according to the power that works in us* (Ephesians 3:20).

Far too many of us begin our Christian lives with the feeling that not only is God not a God of more than enough, but He actually gets satisfaction from making us give up good things. How mistaken can we be? Yet many Christians feel that the only time they are pleasing God is when they are suffering, sacrificing, or giving up something.

This is not the kind of God the Bible reveals to us. The Bible is God's written Word which unfolds His will for you and me. And from Genesis to Revelation the Bible proclaims the story of God's healing power.

El Shaddai is portrayed throughout the Scriptures as a God of abounding, unending love and goodness, who wants to give good gifts to His children. The Words says, *Every good gift and every perfect gift is from above, and comes down from the Father of lights, with whom there is no variation or shadow of turning* (James 1:17).

Sickness is not a gift of God. Sickness cannot be called good; therefore, God cannot be its author. Remember that in the Old Testament story of Job, the Bible specifically points out that he was afflicted at the hand of Satan. And this happened because Job himself said, "The thing I feared has come upon me." Fear opened the door. The fear attack upon Job's family, his prosperity, and his health was not of God. God is absolutely good. There is no evil in Him. And His goodness is revealed to us in the person of His Son, Jesus Christ, who came into the world to show us what God is like.

Once Jesus said to His disciples, *"He who has seen Me has seen the Father"* (John 14:9). If you want to know what God is like, look at Jesus and His ministry. This is why it is important to read the Bible. The Word reveals Jesus and Jesus reveals God to us.

And what kind of ministry did Jesus have upon this earth?

The four Gospels—Matthew, Mark, Luke and John—provide an inspired historical record of Jesus' earthly ministry. When we read about Jesus in the Gospels, we see that He performed one miracle after another … one healing after another.

Jesus said, *"The Spirit of the Lord is upon Me, because He has anointed Me to preach the gospel to the poor. He has sent Me to heal the brokenhearted, to preach deliverance to the captives and recovery of sight to the blind, to set at liberty those who are oppressed"* (Luke 4:18).

And in Acts 10:38 it is written, *"God anointed Jesus of Nazareth with the Holy Spirit and with power, who went about doing good and healing all who were oppressed by the devil, for God was with Him."*

Every waking moment of Jesus' three-year ministry here on earth was dedicated to accomplishing those things.

Jesus said, *"The Son of Man did not come to destroy men's lives but to save them"* (Luke 9:56).

And, *"The thief (the devil) does not come except to steal, and to kill, and to destroy. I have come that they may have life, and that they may have it more abundantly"* (John 10:10).

Actually, most Christians have not understood that God wants them to live an abundant life. Therefore, they have not applied their faith, they have not opened themselves up to receive what God wants them to have.

Everywhere I go I see hundreds of people get healed and delivered. That's part of the ministry God has called me to. But every time I minister to the sick and pray for people to be healed, I realize how much God's people need to be taught about the health and healing that is theirs through faith in *El Shaddai*.

Often, people come to my services and ask me to pray for a particular ailment or physical condition. After I pray, I often ask them if there is anything else they need to be healed of. Many times, to their utter amazement, they discover that God has given them a complete overhaul. Why didn't they ask to be healed of their arthritis, poor vision, deafness, or stomach trouble? They had gotten used to living with it. You should see how happy these people are when they find that God is more than enough—that He has done even more than they hoped for.

Isn't it wonderful that God wants to give us more than we even ask for? That's because He really is *El Shaddai*—the God of more than enough.

God's Word says, *"My people are destroyed for lack of knowledge"* (Hosea 4:6).

In the last few years I have seen literally thousands of men and women healed—even some who were near death—through absolute miracles. But what of the millions of people who are sitting in churches all across America suffering in their bodies simply because they've never been taught that *El Shaddai*—

more than enough for your healing

the God of more than enough—is not only able to heal but to keep them in perfect health.

God promises a full life to His children. *With long life I will satisfy him, and show him My salvation* (Psalm 91:16).

How can we receive that promise? The only condition set forth by *El Shaddai* is to develop a loving relationship with Him. He said, "As you dwell in the secret place of the most high, I'll give you salvation and long life … because you have set your love upon Me" (see verses 1, 14).

God's commandment is, *"You shall love the Lord"* (Matthew 22:37). And when we do what His Word says, we open the door for His blessings to flow.

According to the Bible, sickness came into the world by the disobedience of man. It goes directly back to God's first creation, Adam and Eve. God made them whole, healthy and happy. But man chose to break fellowship with God. He sold out his birthright as the god of this world to satan. And as Adam and Eve fell from their first estate, a curse was upon man, and from that time there has been sickness—in the land, the water, the air, in every person born.

This is why God sent His Son Jesus Christ to the earth to die in our behalf—to go in our place to Calvary to bear our sins and sicknesses.

I once read a story in *Guideposts* about a pastor who was trying to prepare his Christmas Sunday sermon. Although he'd worked hard and spent ample time praying and studying, when Saturday night came … he still had nothing.

As he sat there struggling to find a topic, his housekeeper came into the study. "It's Tommy, sir," she said. "He's under his bed and won't come out."

more than enough

The church operated a small orphanage, and most of the children had been invited to spend Christmas in the homes of various families in the community. All except Tommy. He was a problem child—not because he was unruly or mean but because of his extreme shyness.

The pastor sighed in frustration as he left his study and walked over to the orphanage dormitory. With not even the idea for a sermon, the last thing he needed was to spend time coaxing a youngster out from under a bed!

But that's what he found himself doing. And Tommy wouldn't budge. Watching the other children going off with loving people had made his loneliness even more intense. Knowing he had no place to go and no special person to love him and want him deepened his despondency. Huddled in the darkness beneath his bed, Tommy was almost paralyzed with fear and despair.

The pastor laid down on the floor and talked to the youngster. He tried to tell him how nice Christmas was going to be, with presents to open and good food to eat. There was no response … except an occasional muffled sob. Finally, not knowing what else to do, the minister slid under the bed with Tommy, reached out and pulled the little body into his arms. The youngster snuggled closer and began to relax a bit. Soon he felt comfortable enough to come out into the light.

Suddenly, the pastor's Christmas message exploded in his mind. This was the real meaning of Christmas. The Son of God was born to humble people in a stable, not by accident. He saw the needs of mankind—that people were lost, undone, frightened, and He came down on their level and wrapped His arms of love around them.

more than enough for your healing

So it was that the pastor stood before his congregation on Christmas Sunday and preached about how God came down and crawled under the bed with humanity.

That's what Jesus did for us.

Christ's mission is recorded in three separate verses of Scripture:

> *Surely He has borne our griefs and carried our sorrows; yet we esteemed Him stricken, smitten by God, and afflicted. But He was wounded for our transgressions, He was bruised for our iniquities; the chastisement for our peace was upon Him, and by His stripes we are healed* (Isaiah 63:4, 5).

> *That it might be fulfilled which was spoken by Isaiah the prophet, saying: "He Himself took our infirmities and bore our sicknesses"* (Matthew 8:17).

> *Who Himself bore our sins in His own body on the tree, that we, having died to sins, might live for righteousness—by whose stripes you were healed* (1 Peter 2:24).

Through man's sin and rebellion—by saying, in essence, "God, I don't need You. I'm going to do things my own way"—man brought sickness and suffering upon himself. And now we must turn back to God with an understanding of His will.

If we will open up and start searching the Bible to learn about *El Shaddai* and His ways, understanding that He loves us, He cares for us, and wants us to have His health and healing, we will begin experiencing His miracle-power in our lives.

Healing is part of the Atonement. Your health and healing has already been bought and paid for. It's yours—if you'll only reach out and receive it.

El Shaddai—the God of more than enough—lives within you, and He is bigger than any disease or sickness you will ever face.

Healing is part of your inheritance as God's child.

Here are some steps that will help you receive what God has provided for you:

First, know that God WANTS to heal you.

John expressed God's wish for you. He wrote, *Beloved, I pray that you may prosper in all things and be in health, just as your soul prospers* (3 John 2). *El Shaddai* wants you to have health equal to the health of your soul. He wants to prosper you in your everyday life the same way He wants your soul to prosper. He wants to give you life—ABUNDANT LIFE—so that you may serve Him better and help others.

Second, you must WANT God to heal you.

Jesus said, "I want you to have life and have it abundantly." When you desire healing, you desire what God has promised you. When you ask Him for healing, you are asking for what He has provided for you. You are asking only that God keep His promise, AND HE WILL!

Never say, "I am not receiving because God doesn't want to heal me."

El Shaddai is a more-than-enough God who delights in giving to those who ask Him with a whole heart.

Not only must you want God to heal you—you must want to be healed. That's right—there are people who actually get used to being sick and would not be comfortable if they weren't uncomfortable! Perhaps they enjoy the attention they get from being sick, or have the mistaken notion that their suffering somehow brings glory to God and earns them some kind of merit or divine "points" in Heaven. Nothing could be further from the truth.

If a person really believed his sickness was pleasing to God, why would he go to the doctor for treatment or take medicine in an attempt to get well … and out of God's will? That would defeat the whole point of "suffering for Jesus." The truth is, of course, that God wants us to be healthy and whole.

But you must want to get well if you are to receive a healing touch from God. John's Gospel tells about Jesus confronting a man at the pool of Bethesda who had been sick for 38 years. Do you know what the Lord asked him? He said, *"Do you want to be made well?"* (John 5:6). In other words, "Do you want to be healed and healthy?"

When the man faced up to this question and started focusing on his answer instead of his problem, he was instantly, totally healed.

Third, you must find God's promise for you in the Word and claim it.

There are more than 7,000 specific promises in the Bible. At least one of them—probably several—pertains to you and your present need. Find the Scripture promise that speaks to your spirit and stand on it. Say, "God, this is Your promise, and I know You are bringing it to pass in my life." Every day—

every hour, if necessary—remind yourself of God's promise and expect it to be fulfilled in your life.

You see, there's a Scripture verse for everything.

If you're hemorrhaging or bleeding—and you should not be—you can speak Ezekiel 16:6 ... *"And when I passed by you and saw you struggling in your own blood, I said to you in your blood, 'Live!' Yes, I said to you in your blood, 'Live!'"*

That verse saved my life when I was in a hospital hemorrhaging to death and the doctor could do nothing for me. They had worked over me all day, doing everything that man could do and yet nothing seemed to help. I was considered dead for all practical purposes—they had already drawn the curtain around the bed to isolate me from other patients. It was toward 9:30 in the evening at Methodist Hospital in Dallas, Texas when I remembered Ezekiel 16:6. I said to a friend, "Bring the Bible over and stand next to me and read the verse of Scripture."

She did and I received the Word. I am a good recipient of the Word because I make a decision to do so. You speak God's Word to me and it goes into the very marrow of my bones. IT goes into every cell and particle of my being because I have made myself a receiver of anything that's good. (And you can, too!)

Thirty minutes after my friend came to stand by my bed, I began to sing, "The Lord's my Shepherd, I'll not want. He makes me to lie down in pastures green. He leadeth me by the quiet waters." And I went on and sang the verse.

The people around me—my family—were saying, "Don't sing, you're too weak."

more than enough for your healing

I wouldn't shut up—*I was receiving a healing.*

The devil knew it and tried to kill me. But you see, I'm not a quitter. God didn't intend for me to die. He intended for me to minister the gospel. In 30 minutes all the hemorrhaging stopped! I was well!

From time to time the symptoms of the affliction try to come back upon me, trying to tell me I'm going to die. But every time I stand upon the Word of God. I confess the promise of Isaiah 53:5—*But He was wounded for our transgressions, He was bruised for our iniquities; the chastisement of our peace was upon Him and by His stripes we are healed.* I declare, "I am healed by God's power." And the symptoms have always disappeared.

People sometimes ask, "When I confess that I am healed and there is no apparent change in my condition, isn't that a lie?"

Not at all! I like to look at this within the context of Mark 11:24—*Whatever things you ask when you pray, believe that you receive them, and you will have them.* So if one is not comfortable saying, "I have it," say instead, "I believe I received it!"

I often tell people I pray that the manifestation of their healing will catch up with their confession. We are what we say and think. When we say and think—or confess—what God has already said about us, there will come a point in time when the desired manifestation will come.

It works for me. It will work for you. Because our God is more than enough for our healing and our continued health.

If you need a miracle in your body right now, pray this prayer with me—

Healing God, there is no variation or hint of turning in You. You never change or change Your mind. You said Jesus was wounded for my transgressions ... bruised for my iniquities ... the chastisement of my peace was upon Him ... and with His stripes I was healed. You sent Your beloved Son, Jesus, to pay for perfect wholeness for me and all who accept His life. I reject all fear because You said the thief comes to steal, kill and destroy, but You came to bring me abundant life—God's life! The illness that tries to remain in my body must go in Jesus' Name. Father, I know it isn't Your will for me to be sick and suffer. Therefore, I accept Your Word and its healing power in His wonderful name. Amen.

chapter
five

more than enough for your family

THE FAMILY IS SURELY THE best social concept in the whole world. Of course, that should be no surprise because the idea sprang from the creative mind of God.

When it is working as the Lord intended, the family provides for virtually every need of its individual members. A man and woman find love, fulfillment, and a sense of completeness and well-being as they come together, husband and wife, and become one unit.

After a while a child is born to them. The human baby is perhaps the most helpless and vulnerable creature on the earth, so the new parents do everything in their power to care for it. They keep their baby warm, clothe it, feed it, bathe it, caress it, and surround it with loving care. As it grows, they teach it to walk, talk, and care for itself. Later, they provide their child with an education, and teach the child about God and His relationship to the Heavenly Father.

The family builds a home together that is joyful, secure, productive, and peaceful. Each family member ministers to the others in some way. It's a place where weariness is rested, hunger fed, concerns shared, and problems solved. The family relationship gives life its richest meaning.

Because the family is a divinely ordained institution that is good for mankind, it's not surprising that it is a favorite target of the enemy. Satan unleashes his most vicious attack on the family because it is the living embodiment of God's love to mankind and provides a source of strength and protection against all outside forces. If the devil can break up or disperse the unity of the family, he knows he has weakened each individual—father, mother, brother, sister—and made them more susceptible to failure.

But God has provided for the protection and preservation of the family. And despite all the dire predictions of the prophets of doom in every generation, the family has endured. Because *El Shaddai*—the God of more than enough—wants every family …your family … to prosper and be blessed, spiritually, physically, and financially.

In fact, the first time God revealed Himself as *El Shaddai* in Genesis, it was to pronounce a promise of blessing upon the family of Abram. God said, "I'll give you so many children, so many descendants that from now on your name will even be changed to Abraham—father of many nations." And although Abraham was almost 100, and his barren wife, Sarai, was past 90, *El Shaddai* made them fruitful. In fact, Abraham continued to father children almost until he died at age 175! His family did produce many nations—including Israel.

And *El Shaddai* gave Job a new family after his seven sons and three daughters were killed in a great windstorm. After Job withstood the terrible loss brought about by his fear and still maintained his trust in God, the Lord gave him back double the wealth and possessions he had lost, and restored his family. Job had seven sons and three daughters, just as he had before.

But God gave him even nicer children than he had before! I know, you're probably thinking, "How can you say that? His first seven sons and three daughters were probably very nice!"

No doubt they were. But I think it's kind of interesting that the biblical account doesn't say much about the first set of children. But it does describe the second set—at least the girls. Job 42:15 says, *In all the land were found no women so beautiful as the daughters of Job.*

By the way, *El Shaddai* expressed His divine will regarding the rights of women at least 1,500 years before the time of Christ. In a culture where women were regarded as chattel, with no social standing or legal identity of their own, God gave these women special recognition. He inspired the writer of the Book of Job to even list their names—Jemimah, Keziah, and Keren-Happuch—and to note that their father gave them an inheritance along with their brothers, an unheard of thing for those days!

The Word of God also tells us that the family of Job continued to survive. *After this Job lived one hundred and forty years, and saw his children and grandchildren for four generations. So Job died, old and full of days* (Job 42:16, 17).

I counsel with a great many people who attend my meetings across the nation. Hundreds of people telephone for prayer and guidance, and thousands of others write to my office each month.

Out of all the concerns people share, the most frequently mentioned requests deal with the family. They ask prayer for unhappy marriages, parent-child conflicts, and in-law problems. But above all else, people want to see their loved ones brought to Christ. "How should I go about witnessing to non-Christian family members?" they ask. "Does it do any good to pray for their salvation if they don't want to be saved? Should I not say anything about their wrong behavior to avoid offending them? My children have strayed away from what they were taught—will God bring them back? Do you have any advice for a new Christian on how to share the gospel with his family who are not believers?"

Do any of those questions sound familiar? Are you searching for some of the same answers? Let me share some of my personal experiences with you and offer some Bible-based suggestions that will encourage you in the Lord.

When I found the reality of the Word of God in my own life, I simply exploded into action. I thought the whole world wanted to know what I'd discovered, and I set out to tell them. I was the biggest "mouthpiece" for Jesus you ever saw. All I could do was talk about God—and that's all I talked about.

At that time, I had no concept of being called into the ministry. I couldn't understand why everybody wasn't working for the Lord. I mean, I talked about God to anyone who would listen—I prayed for anything that didn't move away from me.

Some people thought I was strange—that I'd gone off the deep end. Even some of my family, who had been nominally involved in church for many years, thought I was overreacting. But the exuberant, enthusiastic vitality got through to many people, and several of my friends and loved ones had beautiful experiences with the Lord as a result.

But not my brother, Sam. He thought I was strange. He knew about God—he'd even felt the call of God on his life. But he didn't think he could live the life of rigid laws, and he ran from God. He'd had the same experience I had of growing up in a negative atmosphere chafing under a long list of "don'ts" and "thou-shalt-nots."

So he had no intention of responding to the gospel and becoming a committed Christian. He was a traveling salesman … running from God. I was praying for him. Mother was praying for him. Several other friends were praying, too.

Mother gave him a Christian book one day, and Sam took it just to be polite and not hurt her feelings. He tossed it in his briefcase, never intending to read it. But back out on the road, one night he was bored and had nothing to do, so he started reading the book. And it got hold of him.

He went back through Dallas to visit Mother and she took him to a seminar with a minister named Chuck Flynn. During the service, Chuck called Sam out of the audience, and through the power of the Holy Spirit, told him about himself—how old he was when God called him to preach and some other things.

This made an indelible impression on Sam's mind, and he started coming back to the Lord. He got back in church, started having fellowship with believers, and began reading books and literature by great men of God like Kenneth Hagin and Gordon Lindsay. He also got involved with the Full Gospel Businessmen.

I was thrilled. But I still wanted to see Sam go into the ministry and do what God wanted him to do. Everywhere I went—in many churches and prayer meetings I visited—I asked people to pray for Sam.

One day Sam introduced himself to a man at a Full Gospel Businessmen's convention and the fellow said, "Oh, I know you. Vicki told us about you, and we've been praying for you to do what God said."

Sam was kind of upset with me over that! But I kept praying. And in about three months Sam realized he was missing God's will for his life and he felt just miserable. He called mother and said, "I'm going to fast and pray until God shows me what I'm supposed to do."

Three days later I called Sam and invited him to come to Dallas to see me. I didn't know what to tell him, but I'd been praying for him to obey the Lord, and I felt God would show him what to do. Sam came to Dallas, and we had a good visit. One day we were taking a drive on the freeway, and suddenly I said, "If I were you, I know exactly what I'd do!"

"What would you do?"

"I'd sell my house and move to Tulsa, Oklahoma, and go to Rhema Bible Training Center." Brother Hagin was just opening Rhema at that time—they had never had a class.

Well, that's exactly what Sam and his family did. His wife wasn't too enthusiastic at first—after all, they had three teenage boys and many responsibilities. But God led them and worked out the arrangements. And after going through Rhema, thinking all the time he would be a teacher, Sam felt called to be a pastor.

He established one of the most powerful and productive churches in all of New England.

Who knows, perhaps if my personal witness to Sam had been more low-key, more restrained, more dignified, it might have had no effect on him at all. But I was so enthusiastic, so totally hyper, that he couldn't ignore me. He knew what I'd been like before, and he knew something had happened—something real and powerful.

So I don't really have any words of caution or restraint for new Christians who are excited and on fire for God and eager to win their lost loved ones for Jesus.

You see, they're babes in Christ, and they can say and do things a more mature believer might not be able to do. I've seen spiritual babies do too many things and get by with it. Mom and Dad would just grin at baby when he pulled all the books off the shelf and say, "Isn't he sweet? Isn't that cute?" Later on he wouldn't get away with it.

I say, let new converts go and win people to the Lord the best way they know how. They'll "grow up" soon enough!

Another thing to remember is that different people respond to different approaches. The way I witnessed to Sam—just all noise, knees, and elbows—would not be effective with my Aunt Nancy at all. The way I deal with her is to just let her say anything she wants to say, and I calmly accept it. You see, she knows who I am and what God is doing in my life, and she doesn't want me preaching to her. So I don't. I just love her with all that's in me. We get along fine, and nothing she has to say bothers me because I know the Lord is going to draw her right into the kingdom of God. I'm absolutely confident He'll do it, so I don't get anxious and push her into an argument or controversy.

But *El Shaddai*—the God of more than enough—knows just the way to win each individual. And His Word is filled with encouragement and promises concerning the families of the righteous.

Whether your unsaved loved ones are "good people" or really sinful ... whether your past life was spectacularly wicked or just not committed to Christ, you can be a positive influence in winning your family. And God is able and willing to save your entire family. Just don't get discouraged. Never quit believing for their salvation.

You may feel that it is easier to pray for strangers and talk with them about the Lord than it is with your own friends and family. That's not so unusual. The Bible says even Jesus had a difficult time ministering to His family and neighbors.

> *Then He went out from there and came to His own country ... now He could do no mighty works there, except that He laid His hands on a few sick people and healed them. And He marveled because of their unbelief* (Mark 6:1, 5, 6).

You see, the problem was not with Jesus. He could have performed mighty miracles among them just as He did in other towns. The problem was in how the people perceived Him. They thought they knew Him too well. After all, they knew His family ... and they had known Him since He was a child.

> *And when the Sabbath had come, He began to teach in the synagogue. And many hearing Him were astonished, saying, "Where did this Man get these things? And what wisdom is this which is given to Him, that such mighty works are performed by His hands! Is this not the carpenter, the Son of Mary, the brother of James, Joses, Judas, and Simon? Are not His sisters here with us?" And they were offended at Him. But Jesus said to them, "A prophet is not without honor except in his own country, among his own relatives, and in his own house"* (Mark 6:2-4).

You also may be having a hard time sharing God with your family and friends, especially if you led a life that was hard or unloving before you accepted Christ.

One reason for this is because your friends and family know you better than anyone. They've lived with you day after day, and, like the people said of Jesus, they know your brothers and sisters … they know your past. It may be hard for them to accept the fact that you have changed, that you are different than you were before.

Many people have told me that when they first accepted Christ, their families and friends felt that this "religious stuff" was just a phase they were going through. It's pretty hard to convince someone you are sincere about serving God if they dismiss your experience as a "phase." But you can do it through patience and steadfastness over a period of time and by a persistent walk with God.

Another reason the unsaved might not receive you is because darkness is not comfortable in the presence of light. Even without your acting "better" than them, your walk with God makes the unsaved acutely aware of their own needful predicament—and most people don't like to be reminded of this.

When you were living a life of rebellion, your family could use your behavior to somehow justify their own shortcomings. After all, they were not as bad as you. But when you accept Christ and change, their reason for not accepting Him is gone.

Even if you led a good life before accepting Christ, you may find it hard to share Him with your family. You may have been a reasonably happy, well-adjusted, self-sufficient person all your life. And when you find the true meaning of life, the change that takes place inside you may not be spectacularly evident, even to your own family. Again, patience and persistence in your Christ-like way will pay off sooner or later. Be faithful.

A third reason your family might not accept a conversion testimony is if they felt it came too late. This often happens when parents are saved after their children are grown or nearly grown. They sometimes have a hard time forgiving

Mom and Dad for all the years when they weren't serving Christ. Perhaps they feel their parents were cold and unloving, or even mistreated them. They may see the change as a way of parents to try to manipulate them or to somehow make up for a lifetime of wrongs.

No matter what kind of reception you encounter, *El Shaddai* is the God of more than enough for your family. He is able to break down every barrier between you and them and use you to bring them face-to-face with Jesus.

He is ready to save their souls and fill them with the precious Holy Spirit—and also to shower all of His blessings upon them.

While it's true you can't force anyone to accept Christ against their will, you can bring down every hindering force that prevents them from making an objective decision. You can release God's spirit of adoption upon them, and you can be there to strengthen them with the love of God.

God promises us many times in His Word that if we are obedient to Him, He will save our families. Let's look at just a few of these promises:

> *The children of your servants will continue, and their descendants will be established before You* (Psalm 102:28).

> *But the mercy of the Lord is from everlasting to everlasting on those who fear Him, and His righteousness to children's children* (Psalm 103:17).

> *The posterity of the righteous will be delivered* (Proverbs 11:21).

> *I will pour My Spirit on your descendants, and My blessing on your offspring* (Isaiah 44:3).

> *For I will contend with him who contends with you, and I will save your children* (Isaiah 49:25).

more than enough for your family

"Believe on the Lord Jesus Christ, and you will be saved, you and your household" (Acts 16:31).

If any of those close to you are not born into the family of God, believe in these promises right now. Pick out the ones that come alive in your heart and commit them to memory. Remind God of His promise every day. God wants your family—every man, woman, and child in your household and on the face of the earth—to know Jesus as Lord and Saviour. Know that it is His will to save them; that He is *not willing that any should perish but that all should come to repentance* (2 Peter 3:9).

Remember, repentance is not just saying, "I'm sorry for doing this or that" but actually means to turn around and go in another direction. Repentance means turning from one's mistakes and failures to a better way of life.

Your persistent prayers on your family's behalf and a daily, consistent walk with God will bring them to Christ. As they see the change in your life and the new joy and meaning you have found, they too will want to experience it.

It may take a while—the hurts of the past are not easily forgotten—but one day your family will acknowledge that Christ is Lord of your life. Then you will have the opportunity of sharing Christ with them.

The key to winning your family to Christ is continuing obedience to God's will and unwavering faith in God's Word. Trust God to do His part in saving your family and be faithful in doing yours.

What is your part? If you have children at home, you have the responsibility to obey the Lord and live righteously so your children can see by your example what it means to be a Christian. Then they can accept Christ for themselves. God emphasized this parental responsibility to the Israelites when He said through His servant Moses, *"I call heaven and earth as witnesses today against you, that I have set before you life and death, blessing and cursing; therefore choose life, that both you AND YOUR DESCENDANTS may live"* (Deuteronomy 30:19, emphasis added).

You play an important part in helping your children know God so they can live abundant lives now and have eternal lives in Heaven. The Bible specifically tells you what to do so that your children will someday accept Christ.

> *Fathers, do not irritate and provoke your children to anger—do not exasperate them to resentment—but rear them [tenderly] in the training and discipline and the counsel and admonition of the Lord* (Ephesians 6:4, *Amplified Bible*).

Proverbs 22:6 says, *Train up a child in the way he should go, and when he is old he will not depart from it.*

Training means more than instruction. It means firmly requiring them to do right until it becomes natural for them to do it.

In the military service, all new recruits go through basic training. Part of the weapons education begins with the instruction: "This is a rifle. It breaks down into these parts. Practice taking your rifle apart and putting it back together until you know it well enough to assemble it correctly in the dark."

That's the instruction. Now comes the next phase—training. "Take the rifle. Break it down into parts. Now reassemble it until you can do it in the dark."

That's the kind of disciplined training that is necessary in a Christian family.

It's one thing to tell a child about the benefits of tithing, for example. It's another to help him figure out how much of his allowance he will give.

Until your children are old enough to make their own decisions, you must help them make the right choices.

Of course, a vital part of Christian training in the home must be by example as well as by instruction. It doesn't do a lot of good to *tell* your children to live right if you don't *practice* living right yourself. You may not always be perfect, but the God of more than enough will give you the wisdom, strength, and sufficiency you need to raise your children to know Him.

> *"Therefore you shall lay up these words of mine in your heart and in your soul, and bind them as a sign on your hand, and they shall be as frontlets between your eyes. You shall teach them to your children, speaking of them when you sit in your house, when you walk by the way, when you lie down, and when you rise up. And you shall write them on the doorposts of your house and on your gates, that your days and the days of your children may be multiplied"* (Deuteronomy 11:18-21).

I receive many telephone calls and letters from people whose children have run away from home or whose children no longer keep in touch with them. Many times these parents did not accept Christ until after their children were gone, and they wonder if maybe it's too late for them to share Christ with their children.

It makes me happy to be able to tell them that with God it isn't too late. *El Shaddai* is more than able to touch their children's hearts and bring them home. I encourage these parents to claim the promise of Isaiah 43:5, 6—*"Fear not, for I am with you; I will bring your descendants from the east, and gather you from the west; I will say to the north, 'Give them up!' and to the south, 'Do not keep them back!' Bring my sons from afar, and My daughters from the ends of the earth"* (emphasis added). Isn't that marvelous? No matter where your children may be—even if you don't know where they are—God knows about them and will bring them to a place where they have an opportunity to accept Christ. He will love them to His side!

What about a husband or wife who has not accepted Christ? God asks that you do everything you can to live in peace with them so that the power of the Holy Spirit might be free to work in their lives and draw them to Christ.

Nevertheless let each one of you in particular so love his own wife as himself, and let the wife see that she respects her husband (Ephesians 5:33).

If any brother has a wife who does not believe, and she is willing to live with him, let him not divorce her. And a woman who has a husband who does not believe, if he is willing to live with her, let her not divorce him. For the unbelieving husband is sanctified by the wife, and the unbelieving wife is sanctified by the husband (1 Corinthians 7:12-14).

You can trust God for the salvation of your children and for your mate. And should they ever accept Christ and then fall away, He is more than enough to bring them back into right relationship with Him.

"These also who erred in spirit will come to understanding, and those who murmured will learn doctrine" (Isaiah 29:24).

"In returning and rest you shall be saved (Isaiah 30:15).

"Return, you backsliding children, and I will heal your backslidings" (Jeremiah 3:22).

El Shaddai is more than enough for your backslidden loved ones. He is able to quicken and convict the most wayward heart.

God promises to meet every need that your family faces. When the Word of God fills your home, His blessings and promises rest upon everyone there.

more than enough for your family

"Only take heed to yourself, and diligently keep yourself, lest you forget the things your eyes have seen, and lest they depart from your heart all the days of your life. And teach them to your children and your grandchildren." (Deuteronomy 4:9).

You are the one who can determine whether the presence of *El Shaddai* is welcome in your home. So make a clear, firm, unmistakable declaration. Declare with Joshua, *"As for me and my house, we will serve the Lord"* (Joshua 42:15).

David said in Psalm 101:2, *I will walk within my house with a perfect heart.* That is the kind of commitment you need in order to effectively reach your lost loved ones.

Matthew 9:18-25 tells of a little girl raised from the dead on the strength of her father's faith in Jesus. The Syrophoenician woman in Mark 7:25-30 is another example of a parent whose faith brought about her daughter's deliverance.

I encourage you to pray for your family and friends, be a faithful witness before them, and claim God's promises for their eventual salvation. You can even claim God's promises for their protection and health. I have received many letters from people who stood on the promises of Psalm 91 for the protection of their loved ones, and God has honored their faith.

Your intercession and faithfulness usher in the miraculous for your family and friends. Your steadfastness is their key to receiving salvation—and the very best—from *El Shaddai*, the God of more than enough.

Let this be your prayer today—

Father, You said You are not willing that any should perish but that all should come to repentance. I come on behalf of my family. Gather them from the East, from the West and keep not back, bring my sons and daughters from the ends of the earth into Jesus. Thank You Lord for pouring out Your Spirit upon my descendants. I confess Your faithfulness in causing the hearts of my family to turn to You. Salvation is mine! My family is coming into Your care, confessing Jesus as Lord. Amen.

Vicki Jamison-Peterson

Her Life, Her Love, Her Legacy

more than enough

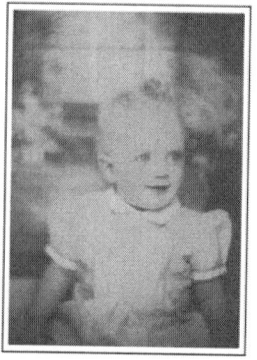  

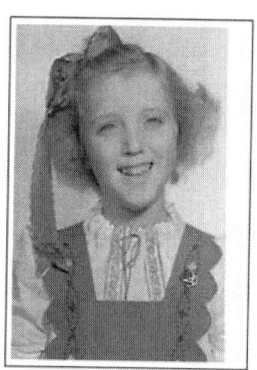  

Vicki Jamison-Peterson—Her Life, Her Love, Her Legacy

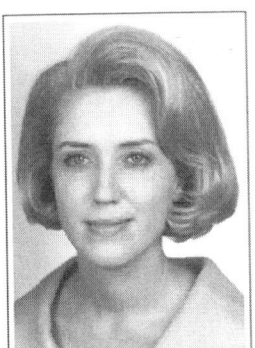

more than enough

family

Victor and Ruthe
Smith with
brother Sam & Vicki

Vicki with
brother Sam and
father Victor Smith
1950

Vicki and
sister Julie Avary
1971

Vicki Jamison-Peterson—Her Life, Her Love, Her Legacy

Vicki with mother Ruthe Lamb
1982

Vicki with brother Sam Smith and mother Ruthe Lamb
1988

Vicki, mother Ruthe Lamb, Judy Upjohn, Houston and Tar
1998

Vicki with sister Julie Avary and Jean Fowler (friend)
2005

Praise the Lord
PTL
Television Broadcast

Greg Smith (nephew) assisting

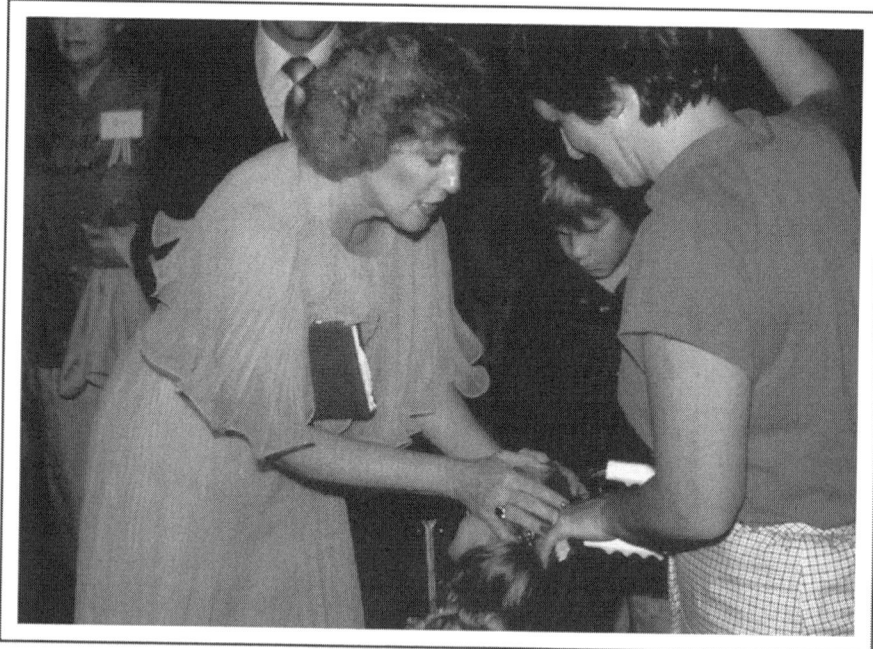

Vicki at PTL with Uncle Henry, Jim and Tammy Bakker

Vicki at PTL

Vicki at PTL with Jim Bakker

Ministry

Vicki with brother Sam Smith, and Kenneth Hagin
1977

Vicki at TBN with Paul and Jan Crouch
1978

Vicki with Fern and Phil Halverson
1979

Vicki on the set of Channel 38 in Chicago
1979

Vicki and Donna Douglas
"Ellie Mae" of the "Beverly Hillbillies"
1982

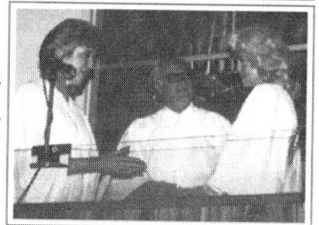

Vicki baptizing Donna Douglas
Phil Halverson assisting
1982

Vicki and Buddy Harrison

Vicki and David Ingles 1983

Vicki 1985

Vicki with Jim and Lori Bakker 2003

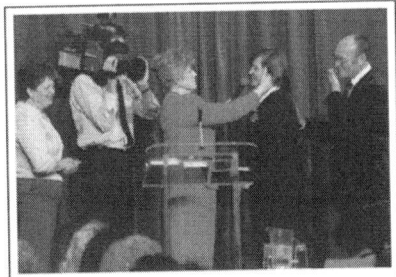
Vicki 1986

Vicki 1985

Vicki 1986

more than enough

Staff

Vicki and Staff
1975

Vicki and Staff
1978

Vicki's Staff
1979

Vicki and Staff
1981

Vicki Jamison-Peterson—Her Life, Her Love, Her Legacy

Friends

Vicki at the Dove Awards
1975

Vicki and Sharon Bell-Stromley
1977

Vicki with Barbara and Steve Arbo
1979

Sharon Stromley, Jeanne Kornhaber-Tatum, Vicki and Judy Upjohn
1986

Judy Upjohn, Vicki, mother Ruthe Lamb, Sharon Bell-Stromley and Rex Bronnenberg
1988

Visiting La La Land
1988

La La Land
1988

Vicki with Rev. Carol and Dr. Bill Cooper
1992

Vicki and Lucy McKee
2001

Vicki with her Pastors Mark and Janet Brazee
2002

The "Sparkies"
1998

Gloria Copeland, Lucy McKee, Lynne Hammond, Trina Hankins, Brenda Steen, Vicki, Billye Brim and Patsy Cameneti

"I'm just a handmaiden of the Lord, I hold open the curtain and allow the Holy Spirit to do the work."

~ *Vicki Jamison-Peterson*

"Repent ye therefore, and be converted, that your sins may be blotted out, **when the times of refreshing shall come from the presence of the Lord.**"

~ *Acts 3:19 KJV*

chapter six

more than enough for your finances

I LIVE AN ABUNDANT LIFE.

Really, I do.

I refuse to just barely get by in any area of my life.

I have abundant health. My Father doesn't want me to feel worn out and miserable, forcing myself to keep going, dragging through the day. I feel good! I have plenty of energy to do my work and still feel like enjoying life and having fellowship with my friends.

I have an abundant career. I mean, I enjoy what I do. It's the most exciting, satisfying, fulfilling work I can imagine. And the job God has given me to do has grown into a ministry bigger and more far-reaching than I ever dreamed. I'm always eager to get to my next miracle service to see what will happen there. And in each instance, it's always something bigger and better and more exciting than I expected.

more than enough

I enjoy financial abundance. You may say, "I didn't know you were so wealthy." I didn't say I was. In fact, my bank balance and net worth figures would probably alarm most accountants. But I always have everything I need ... and more.

For example, I live in the most beautiful and comfortable house—it's my dream home. By human standards, there is no way I could afford to own it. But my Father worked it all out for me. I have good food to eat—whatever I want. I never have to miss a meal unless I choose to. I drive a comfortable, reliable automobile—it's not elaborate or expensive, but it gets me where I want to go. If I wanted a better car, God would give it to me, but vehicles don't mean a great deal to me.

I do enjoy clothes, though. I like to look nice. I'm constantly appearing before large audiences. It's important that I have clothes that are quality and tasteful. I desire to represent my calling well. And God provides for me.

Once I scheduled a trip—by faith—to the garment district in Los Angeles to buy some new clothes. I didn't have enough money to go—as a matter of fact, I didn't have any money. But I went ahead and made plans for my shopping trip. Because I live abundantly—abundant means that whatever I need or desire is there—all I have to do is ask God, the All-Sufficient one, to provide.

So I began to pray. I said, "Father, I really would like to get some new clothes. I don't necessarily *need* them ... it's not an emergency, but I'm tired of wearing my old ones so often. Please provide the money I need to go shopping. Thank you, Father."

more than enough for your finances

Within two hours, a minister friend walked up to me at the TV studio and handed me an envelope. He said, "This is not a gift for the ministry—it's for you personally." I opened the envelope and there was a check for $700!

That's abundance! That's more than enough. You see, God is elaborate to me. But the secret is that I'm elaborate with God. Everything I have is His, so everything He has is mine. That's how I always have abundance.

I give myself away—my every waking moment belongs to God and to doing His work. And God gives Himself back to me—Himself and what He has—which is enough, and some to spare, for all my needs and desires.

Oh, that's right—I said "desires." God gives me more than just the necessities. Just enough wouldn't be the abundance, you see.

Let me show you what I mean. A few years ago, I found a cologne that I liked. It was just right for me—I wanted to wear it every day. And I did, although it was much more expensive than any cologne I'd ever used before.

I got a small bottle, and before long it was almost used up. "Lord, I need some more cologne," I prayed. And just as I ran out, someone gave me a new bottle. It was exactly the same fragrance, same brand—just a larger bottle!

The cologne situation got almost funny. Individuals would call my secretary and say, "We'd like to get a little gift for Vicki to let her know how much we appreciate her. What would you suggest?" Judy would say, "Well, I know she likes cologne."

This brand was difficult to find, and sometimes the people didn't even ask Judy what I wore. Yet every gift of cologne I received was my brand! At one time, I had four or five bottles stockpiled.

One man I'd helped with some business transactions asked if he could buy me a gift. He took me to a store and asked the clerk to bring out the largest bottle of my favorite cologne she had in stock. It cost almost $150. When I got home, I said, "Lord, that's enough! No more, please."

I do not mean to suggest that God's blessings are capricious and can be manipulated by selfish whims. God is not a vending machine that delivers any item you want if you put enough coins in the slot and push the right button. That's not what I'm saying at all.

But neither is He so limited or stingy that He reluctantly doles out just enough to keep you going, acting all the while as though meeting your needs would bankrupt Heaven. He is a God of abundance ... the Lord of the surplus.

The story of Job is a perfect example of this. The Bible makes it clear that Job was a wealthy and prosperous man. He had more of everything than he really needed. His possessions included 7,000 sheep, 3,000 camels, 500 yoke of oxen (that's 1,000), 500 donkeys ... *and a very large household, so that this man was the greatest of all the people of the East* (Job 1:3).

We've already looked at what happened to Job at the hand of Satan—how he lost all his wealth, all his possessions, and his 10 children, too. And if the story ended there, it would be a good argument that prosperity is bad, that wealth is somehow evil, and that having too much can only bring trouble. One could even say that, although God didn't cause Job's tribulations, He didn't approve of Job's wealth and allowed it to be taken from him.

But the story doesn't end there. Chapter 42 says that Job ended up with twice as many possessions as he had before—14,000 sheep, 6,000 camels, 1,000 yoke of oxen (that's 2,000), and 1,000 donkeys. That sounds like an abundance to me, doesn't it to you? That's a surplus—more than enough. And do you know where it all came from? God gave it to him. The Bible says specifically and unmistakably—*Now the Lord blessed the latter days of Job more than his beginning* (Job 42:12). I'm convinced that if God hadn't wanted Job to have an abundant supply, He wouldn't have given it to him.

But it pleased God to bless Job. And it pleases Him to bless you, too. It actually makes Him happy to give you what you ask for. That's right—I said that blessing you with abundance makes God happy. The Old Testament says, "*Let the Lord be magnified, who has pleasure in the prosperity of His servant*" (Psalm 35:27). And the New Testament says, "*Do not fear, little flock, for it is your Father's good pleasure to give you the kingdom*" (Luke 12:32).

The truth I want you to believe and come to a new understanding of in this chapter is that *El Shaddai*—the God of more than enough—wants you to prosper financially. Why should a child of God—a joint heir with Jesus Christ—be limited in resources and not be able to pay his bills? The God of more than enough promises to meet your needs.

Real prosperity begins in the soul. Jesus said, "*But seek first the kingdom of God and His righteousness, and all these things shall be added to you*" (Matthew 6:33). Just as God saves your soul, re-creates your spirit, and heals your body, He wants to prosper you. **And God's prosperity relates to more than just finances.** It relates to all areas of your life—your relationships, your home, your marriage, your job, your health, your spiritual life ... AND your finances.

Christians can be much more than mere survivors of the national economy. They do not have to be affected like the world and go around with the "my goodness, the interest rates are high" and "times are hard" and "jobs are so difficult to find" blues. There is a workable faith for finances, and it's found in God's Word.

When you DO God's Word, you activate spiritual laws that have been ordained and established from the foundation of the world.

In the beginning, God said that as long as the earth remains there will be "seedtime and harvest" (Genesis 8:22). The apostle Paul referred to this spiritual law—the law of sowing and reaping:

> *Do not be deceived, God is not mocked; for whatever a man sows, that he will also reap* (Galatians 6:7).

> *He who sows sparingly will also reap sparingly, and he who sows bountifully will also reap bountifully. So let each one give as he purposes in his heart, not grudgingly or of necessity; for God loves a cheerful giver. And God is able to make all grace abound toward you, that you, always having all sufficiency in all things, have an abundance for every good work* (2 Corinthians 9:6-8).

The Bible here is talking to Christians who are following the Champion of our faith—Jesus. He didn't sow sparingly or grudgingly. He was the greatest giver the world has ever known.

But, you say, "What about Jesus? Wasn't He poor?"

Let's look at the "poverty" of Jesus. The religious world for generations has portrayed Jesus as a pauper. However, we should take a closer look at Jesus' life before we make Him a pauper. The Word tells us that whatever poverty Jesus knew, He experienced it vicariously. He voluntarily gave up all the wealth of Heaven for the poverty of earth FOR OUR SAKES!

> *For you know the grace of our Lord Jesus Christ, that though He was rich, yet for your sakes He became poor, that you through His poverty might become rich* (2 Corinthians 8:9).

Now, what does "poor" mean? Perhaps we can answer that by defining "prosperity." I believe prosperity means the ability to use God's ability, power, and resources to meet the needs of mankind. It means having enough to further the work of God's kingdom with plenty left over to take care of all your own needs. It means having "more than enough!"

With that definition of prosperity in our thinking, let's review Jesus' ministry. Jesus understood perfectly the statement in the Word, *The earth is the Lord's, and all its fullness* (Psalm 24:1).

He knew that man really "owned" nothing. It all belonged to God. So, living as a man, He did what man was supposed to do. He was our example. Therefore, He became a steward of the resources God made available to Him.

You see, we don't have to "own" things before they can be used for God. When I began my first TV program in Dallas, called "It's a New Day," local dress shops would lend me clothes to wear. A shop of interior design would let us use lush accessories for the set. We got all the benefit of these things with none of the cost. That's prosperity!

And we see the same principles at work in Jesus' ministry. Material goods were provided by friends and followers who believed in what He was doing, who respected Him, and who were acting in obedience to the Holy Spirit.

more than enough

The boat that Jesus used as a platform to speak to the multitudes … the donkey on which He rode into Jerusalem … the room that was used for the last supper—all were loaned to Jesus by people who shared His vision.

The crowning tribute was the borrowed tomb of Joseph of Arimathea. Here was a man of wealth—a pious Jew—who cared enough to give Jesus his own family's resting place.

And let's take a look at Jesus' "crusade team." For three and a half years, Jesus traveled with 12 rugged men—some with families back home to support. No pauper could take care of that travel budget. Yet Jesus always had "more than enough."

The answer is found in Luke 8:1-3:

> *Now it came to pass, afterward, that He went through every city and village, preaching and bringing the glad tidings of the kingdom of God. And the twelve were with Him, and certain women who had been healed of evil spirits and infirmities—Mary called Magdalene, out of whom had come seven demons, and Joanna the wife of Chuza, Herod's steward, and Susanna, and many others* WHO PROVIDED FOR HIM FROM THEIR SUBSTANCE.

You see, Jesus had "faith partners," too! Just as this ministry is supported largely by friends who have been born again, healed, blessed, or ministered to in some way, so Jesus' ministry was underwritten by concerned friends.

Jesus knew He was the Son of God. The earth and the fullness thereof were His. Once He sent a disciple to the Sea of Galilee to catch a fish with a piece of money in its mouth to pay their taxes, demonstrating that He held the keys to all God's abundance in Heaven and earth. Jesus was the God of more than enough and He freely used His resources for Himself and His followers. And that includes you. Remember Jesus' words in Mark 10:29, 30 ...

> *"Assuredly, I say to you, there is no one who has left house or brothers or sisters or father or mother or wife or children or lands, for My sake and the gospel's who shall not receive a hundredfold NOW IN THIS TIME."*

God promises to meet your need **NOW ... IN THIS TIME.** You won't need your financial problems solved in Heaven—you won't have any! God's blessings are for you today.

How do you receive them? By doing His Word ... by allowing *El Shaddai*—the God of more than enough—to operate freely in your life. The secret of receiving is giving in faith. Jesus said, *"Give, and it will be given to You: good measure, pressed down, shaken together, and running over will be put into your bosom. For with the same measure that you use, it will be measured back to you"* (Luke 6:38).

Doesn't that excite you? Jesus said if you give, you will get it back MULTIPLIED ... ABUNDANTLY! Now, I can't tell you how God is going to bring it back to you. That's the adventure of it. It may come in the least likely way, but it will come.

You see, it's a spiritual principle. Whatever you release into the spiritual world always returns to you. When you bind up one area of your life, it binds you up all over. And when you break free in one area, your whole life will become freer.

Do you know that the quickest way to bind up your finances is to stop giving? It shuts all sorts of doors. You get bound up and frightened. And the more you think, "I've got to hoard and hang on to what I've got," the more you build a wall around you that cuts you off from God's blessing.

I have found that the best thing for me to do when I have a financial need is to increase my giving. If I need more, I give more. If my need is big, I give big. I literally give my way out of trouble.

You may ask, "Vicki, how can you afford to do that when your ministry needs thousands of dollars every day?"

The truth is, I can't afford *not* to give!

And neither can you.

When you open your mind to prosperity, things begin to happen. When you say, "Lord, I just love giving to people," people start giving to you.

I love to give. It's so much fun, I can't wait to do it. I go home and clean out my closet and give clothes away. I give money away. I give time and love away.

When I have a need, I give so God can multiply it back to me to meet my need.

Whatever you need, give it away. You want new furniture? Give your old furniture away. You need money? Give money away. You want people to love you? Then give your love away first.

START WHERE YOU ARE AND TAKE A STEP FORWARD. Use the faith you have to believe for what you need. I started by giving $5, $10, $20. I remember when I first faced the challenge of $50. I gave it and believed in faith that God would multiply it back to me "good measure, pressed down, shaken together, and running over."

more than enough for your finances

When I started in this ministry, I believed for one sandwich ... a tank of gas ... a dress ... a pair of shoes ... everything. I took one step at a time. I extended myself a little more each day. I would stretch my faith a little beyond where it had been. I would believe God for a little more and I would give a little more.

That's the way our faith and our giving and our blessings grow. As we grow in our giving and our prosperity, we find out what our level of faith is and what we are responsible for. Then, we take a step beyond that in faith.

Perhaps you've been taught that you're not supposed to receive anything in return when you give. You thought you were being humble when you said, "I don't want anything back. I don't expect." But that does not agree with God's Word.

Malachi 3:10, 11 issues a challenge.

> *"Bring all the tithes into the storehouse, that there may be food in My house, and PROVE ME NOW IN THIS," says the Lord of hosts, "If I will not open for you the windows of heaven and pour out for you such blessing that there will not be room enough to receive it. And I will rebuke the devourer for your sakes, so that he will not destroy the fruit of your ground, nor shall the vine fail to bear fruit for you in the field," says the Lord of hosts.*

When you activate God's spiritual laws, the response is just as sure as knowing that when you throw a ball in the air it must come down.

God has so many ways to lead His children into prosperity. Perhaps it's by leading you to bargains, or sending you unexpected raises, or a part-time job, or a new position. The steps you must take to achieve release from your financial bondage may not seem to be easy—in the beginning or later—but all God requires is what you can do.

Some people give God a tip and expect to receive His best. But God's plan doesn't work that way. If you can give $50 and you give a dollar, you're giving God a tip. But if a dollar is all you've got, that's as big in God's eyes as the wealthy person's gift of a thousand.

Your money represents you. You worked for it. You labored for it. You sweat for it. You put in the hours for it. And when you give a seed-gift, you're giving, literally, a part of your life. You're putting a little bit of your life in God's work. You're giving yourself. And that's what God really wants—YOU.

When you give to God, it's like planting a seed in the ground. That's what God causes to grow.

What you give is what God can take and multiply back to you. If you give nothing, nothing multiplied is still nothing. But when you give God your best, He gives back His best to you—

good measure

pressed down,

and shaken together,

and running over—

MORE THAN ENOUGH!

God says, "I'm going to rebuke the devourer (the devil) at your door, financially. You've been praying for a financial miracle. Step out now and prove Me.

more than enough for your finances

Put something in My hands that I can work with, and I'll give it back to you many times over."

That's how *El Shaddai*—the God of more than enough—will minister to your needs today. He's waiting right now for you to turn your problems over to Him … to put Him to the test. The only place in all of the Bible we're told to test God is in regard to His reward for our giving. We are not to put God to any other test. But we can ask God to prove Himself by pouring His blessings into our lives as we give our tithes and offerings.

Be sure you're obeying God's law of tithing.

Be sure you're giving out of your need to receive what you need.

Be sure you're ready to receive more than enough, an abundance, a surplus!

Father, thank You for being "More Than Enough" for me and everyone else on planet earth!

Now let's pray together—

Father, now that I know that it won't bankrupt Heaven to not only meet my needs but give me some things that aren't necessities, I rejoice. I have been giving, and You said it would be given back to me—good measure, pressed down, shaken together, and running over ... that men would give into my bosom. You also said You would rebuke the devourer for my sake, that You would open the windows of Heaven and pour out a blessing that there should not be room enough to receive it. You said I should lend and not borrow and that I would be a delight to you. Father, Satan's power is broken over my finances in Jesus' Name, and the angels are busy causing avenues of finances to open up and cross my path. I receive abundance because You promised to meet all of my needs according to Your riches in Glory in Christ Jesus. Amen.

chapter seven

more than enough for your weaknesses

EL SHADDAI—THE GOD OF more than enough—is stronger than your every weakness. Have you ever heard someone stand up in a church service and request, "Please pray for me that I'll hold out and be faithful until the end."

Let me tell you a secret. You can't defeat Satan on your own. As long as you're struggling, trying to overcome the enemy in your own power, you will live a defeated life. But by drawing upon the strength of *El Shaddai*, you can conquer every challenge and overcome every weakness.

The heavy burdens that weigh you down are the ones you carry inside you. You can only deal with them through the power of the Holy Spirit. It is the anointing that breaks the yoke of that inner bondage.

Psychiatrists' offices today are filled with people who are facing life and death struggles against fear, guilt, and loneliness. Yet from outer appearances, you might never suspect they were in trouble.

EL SHADDAI is stronger than fear

A businessman seems to have everything ... position, family, home, cars, money ... and yet, he is plagued with fear of failure.

A young mother is overwhelmed by her family responsibilities. Fear crushes her in a vise-like grip as she finds she is unable to cope with life's pressures.

A teenager has gone too far in experimenting with drugs, sex, and alcohol. Underneath a macho exterior, he is scared, uncertain, and confused.

Fear is the most common crippler of the inner man. His symptoms can vary from shortness of breath to blindness.

This is why Jesus confronted human need so often by commanding, "Fear not." He knew He must deal first with the enemy of faith. Once fear was controlled, He could calm the storm and heal the hurt that had caused them to be afraid. His peace caused the icy, hurtful grip of fear to be loosed and new confidence and assurance to rise up in its place.

God's Word tells us to be anxious for nothing, that "perfect love casteth out fear." That perfect love is in Jesus.

I have discovered that these are problems that plague thousands of people in our world today ... even believers struggle against these weaknesses. But fear, guilt, and loneliness need not cripple our lives and ruin our effectiveness in living the life of God. *El Shaddai* is a source of strength we can draw from again and again. Let's look at how His strength can help overcome these weaknesses.

The key to victory over fear is found in Ephesians 6:10—*Finally, my brethren, be strong in the Lord.* You see, it doesn't even mention anything about your own strength. It says, "*Be strong in the Lord.*"

more than enough for your weaknesses

It is just that simple. You must choose this day whom you will follow. If you are God's child and are following Him each day, you can breathe easy and begin to rejoice, for 2 Timothy 1:7 declares, *For God has not given us a spirit of fear, but of power and of love and of a sound mind.*

You can live a full, happy, abundant life … full of faith and free from fear! This is what *El Shaddai*—the God of more than enough—wants for you. The torments of fear are not of God, but of the enemy.

God loves you and wants your life to be abundant. The enemy wants you to suffer and be destroyed. John 10:10 sets the record straight once and for all: "*The thief* (Satan) *does not come except to steal, and to kill, and to destroy. I* (Jesus) *have come that they may have life, and that they may have it more abundantly.*"

The Truth of John 10:10

The thief (Satan) offers you …	Jesus offers you abundant life …
Fear	Faith
Sickness	Healing
Loneliness	Hope
Hopelessness	Belonging
Poverty	Prosperity
Turmoil	Peace
Sorrow	Joy
Hate	Love

You must establish this truth in your heart and life. Then when trouble comes, you'll know who is causing it, and who is your Answer to those problems.

Don't ever blame God for your problems. You can rejoice in the fact that He will take the problems you are experiencing and cause them to work for your own good as his child.

El Shaddai—the God of more than enough—is your Fortress and your Strength against the problem.

You need never cower again under the cruel threats of fear. Go in the strength of the Lord. Your oppressors which once seemed like Goliaths will fall before you like straw men. You can declare triumphantly with David of old, "The battle is the Lord's."

EL SHADDAI is stronger than guilt

In today's permissive society, the problem of guilt has reached epidemic proportions. Society may say virtually any kind of behavior is acceptable, but deep inside men and women know that isn't true.

Too often even believers go on laboring under the awful bondage of guilt which keeps them living in constant fear. Yet they seem unaware of their need to be reconciled to God. Their lack of knowledge of God's loving laws, which are for our protection and good, keep individuals in the clutches of guilt. Also, guilt consciousness prevails in the church world because of misinterpretations of the laws of cause and effect and of the nature of God.

more than enough for your weaknesses

It is impossible to even imagine how many lives are kept unfulfilled and unsettled because of guilt—real or imagined. The human spirit is painfully aware of falling short of the great purpose God has for each life.

Whether caused by genuine guilt, a short-coming, or some failure to measure up to God's standards, no child of God needs to be enslaved by self-oppression.

El Shaddai—the God of more than enough—offers you pardon, mercy and release from all Satan's bondage. His love brings you freedom. No longer will you have to be hoodwinked by the devil. He may try to bully you, enslave you, and make you feel inferior and unworthy. But as you speak the Word of God and declare His truth, Satan must flee!

I once heard an interesting little illustration that depicts the problem of guilt in a graphic way. It involves two youngsters, Johnny and Mary, who were staying for the summer with their grandparents on the farm.

One day, Johnny's habit of throwing stones got him into trouble. Mary dared him to see how close he could throw a rock to old Mollie, Grandma's pet goose. Winding up, he let the stone go, hit right on target … and the goose fell over dead!

Both children knew that Mollie was very special to their Grandma. And Johnny's face turned white as he thought of the consequences. In a panic, he grabbed a shovel, dug a hole behind the barn and buried Mollie.

That evening, before supper, Grandma asked Mary to get the newspaper from the mailbox. As soon as Mary got outside, she announced to her brother, "Johnny, go out to the mailbox and get the newspaper for Grandma."

"But Grandma asked you to do it. It's your job," he said indignantly.

"Johnny," she said, "what about the goose? I'll tell Grandma …"

Without saying another word, Johnny jumped to his feet and ran to get the newspaper. He had already become a slave of his own guilt.

After supper, Grandma said, "Mary, I'd like for you to sweep the front porch."

Johnny tried to hide, but Mary was right behind him. "Johnny," she said in mock sweetness, "Grandma wants you to sweep the front porch."

"I'm not going to do it …" But his words trailed away, and he went off to get the broom. Mary had the upper hand.

This went on for days. When Grandma missed her pet goose and asked if they had seen Mollie, they both acted innocent … Johnny because of his guilt and Mary because of the power her knowledge gave her over her brother.

One evening, Grandpa decided to drive into town and invited the kids to join him. Mary was quick to say yes, but Johnny stayed at home. By now, he was feeling bad all over.

When the car was out of sight, Johnny decided to make his move. With his head down, he wandered in to the sewing room where Grandma was seated in her favorite rocking chair.

"Grandma … I … I have something to tell you," he murmured.

"Yes, what is it, Johnny?"

"You asked me about Mollie, and I didn't tell you the truth …" Johnny's eyes filled with tears as he blurted out his confession.

"I was throwing a rock last Friday and it hit her. I didn't mean to kill her … honest, Grandma."

more than enough for your weaknesses

By now, he was sobbing. "I-I-I'm sorry, Grandma … so sorry. I buried her out back of the barn. Please forgive me."

Grandma took off her glasses, put her sewing down, and reached out to take Johnny on her lap. "Johnny, Grandma forgives you. I'm sure it was an accident … you didn't mean to kill old Mollie. Everything's going to be all right. We'll get another goose."

Grandma wiped away Johnny's tears … and he bounded out the door, relieved and happy again.

Just then, Mary came running up the front steps and into the house. After a few minutes, she was out again, commanding Johnny this time to wash the dishes for Grandma.

"I'm not going to do it. Grandma told you to do it!"

"Johnny," she threatened, "what about the goose?"

Rising to his full stature and with confidence spelled across his smiling face, Johnny said, "What *about* the goose?"

His confession and Grandma's forgiveness had set him free. He was no longer a slave!

This little story is a graphic illustration of how Christ's forgiveness frees us from the guilt and death penalty of sin. Romans 8:1 says, *There is therefore now no condemnation to those who are in Christ Jesus, who do not walk according to the flesh, but according to the Spirit.*

Whatever you are facing, whatever you are troubled with, take the good advice of the old gospel song that says, "Take your burden to the Lord and leave it there."

Rejoice that the Lord has taken that terribly heavy burden off your back. You no longer need to carry it everywhere you go. All things have become new! (see 2 Corinthians 5:17).

EL SHADDAI is stronger than loneliness

A famous doctor was asked to name the worst disease of our day. "Loneliness," he said, "just plain loneliness." Then he went on to say, "The longer I practice, the more sure I am that there is no condition so universal. Everybody, at one time or another, is subject to its blight ... melancholy, bored, forlorn, friendless. And as far as I know, there is nothing doctors can do to cure it."

How many people do you know who are afflicted with the silent, sad suffering of loneliness? Has its dark hurt ever touched your life? Is there a cure for loneliness? Yes, for there are those who have faced banishment, solitary confinement, even actual torture, and lived victoriously through it all.

What is their secret? What is the secret of those who live alone today but have found victory over loneliness?

They have won the battle by seeking God and appropriating His promises. In Him they have found strength and courage to rise above the discouragement of being left alone.

Actually, Christians are never alone, for Jesus said, "I am with you always." He will fill the lonely hours with His wonderful Presence!

El Shaddai—the God of more than enough—has promised to meet every need of your life. You need never feel lonely again!

more than enough for your weaknesses

Lay hold of His promises and apply them to your life.

You can have the peace of God right now, as you accept and believe that *the peace of God, which surpasses all understanding, will guard your hearts and minds through Christ Jesus* (Philippians 4:7).

This peace is promised to all His children: *"Peace I leave with you. My peace I give to you; not as the world gives do I give to you. Let not your heart be troubled, neither let it be afraid"* (John 14:27).

As you open your heart to God, you will find yourself also reaching out to others. One of the best ways to be completely free of loneliness is to become interested in the welfare of others.

There are people who need you. They need your love … desperately. Reach out and be an extension of God's love to someone who needs you.

God is bigger than your weaknesses. There is nothing you are facing that He cannot master.

The same provision He made for the heroes of the faith in both the Old and New Testaments, He promises to you: *"Behold, I give you the authority to trample on serpents and scorpions, and over all the power of the enemy, and NOTHING SHALL BY ANY MEANS HURT YOU"* (Luke 10:19).

Nothing! No sickness … no temptation … no circumstance … no weakness shall harm you as long as you trust in *El Shaddai*.

David knew the secret to victory. He faced mighty Goliath and said, *"This day the Lord will deliver you into my hand, and I will strike you and take your head from you. And this day I will give the carcasses of the camp of the Philistines to the birds of the air and the wild beasts of the earth, that all the earth may know that there is a God in*

Israel. Then all this assembly shall know that the Lord does not save with sword and spear; for the battle is the Lord's, and He will give you into our hands" (1 Samuel 17:46-47).

That's how you can talk to circumstances when you've got Jesus on your side!

So we can say with David, *The Lord is the strength of my life; of whom shall I be afraid?* (Psalm 27:1).

And we can follow Joel's command—*"Let the weak say, 'I am strong'"* (Joel 3:10).

El Shaddai—the God of more than enough—is here to strengthen you in your times of weakness. Lean heavily upon Him, fully trusting in His ability and in His strength, for in His presence is fullness of joy (see Psalm 16:11). Know that because of what Christ has done for you, you are in right standing with God.

Don't be ashamed when you feel weak. Romans 8:1 says, *There is therefore now no condemnation to those who are in Christ Jesus.*

But rather, rejoice that *El Shaddai* is with you, ready to help you overcome your weakness.

Let's pray together—

Father, Source of all strength, I have felt so weak, physically, mentally, financially, and spiritually. Now that I know that feelings have nothing to do with faith, I am placing these "old ways" in the past and I now believe Your Word. You said, "Let the weak say, 'I'm strong.'" My strength comes from You, Lord. Yesterday's mistakes have no power over me. I am not weak. I can do all things in Christ Jesus. I am a new creature in Christ and I do walk according to the Spirit. Lord, You are always with me ... You are a constant companion ... You fill in the void of loneliness. Your presence comforts me. You left Your peace with me and in Your care nothing shall by any means hurt me. The battle is Yours, Lord—we win! In Jesus' Name, Amen.

chapter eight

more than enough for your circumstances

LIFE HAS A WAY OF throwing you for a loop at times. Things can be going along smoothly when, out of the blue, the whole world seems to fall apart. Circumstances come crashing in on you. Disappointments strike. Suddenly, instead of being in control of your life, you find yourself being pushed rudely into a corner ... seemingly at the mercy of forces beyond your control.

Has anything like that ever happened to you?

Have the events and happenings of daily living ever built up like a wall around you until you felt you just couldn't cope with them any more? Most of us have experienced this kind of frustration from time to time, especially when we try to make it in our own strength without consciously drawing upon the unlimited power of *El Shaddai*—the God of more than enough.

more than enough

Our sense of loss, or disappointment, can be caused by many different situations. It could be the tragic loss of a loved one. A close friend may let you down, or the plans you are pursuing suddenly fall through. You may suffer a crushing blow to your own self-esteem, or the pressures of financial problems can be a source of mounting frustration.

Sometimes we brace ourselves for the big blows and make it through the trial, only to be tripped up by some petty annoyance. When pressures accumulate and build up, sometimes what appears to be a very small thing serves as the straw that breaks the camel's back. The great preacher, Dr. R.A. Torrey, once told of a woman who faced the loss of her husband and demonstrated such faith in God through the loss that all her friends marveled at her strength. But this same woman went all to pieces on Monday morning when her clothesline broke just after she had hung up her clean laundry!

Big or small, circumstances can threaten to overwhelm us and eat away at our confidence. If we aren't alert, we can find ourselves suddenly thrown out of focus with life, haunted by doubts about the future … about ourselves … even about God.

But I have great news for you. *El Shaddai*—the God of more than enough—is already on the scene of your dilemma and ready to set you free. He is more than enough to give you victory over every circumstance, every disappointment, every loss you may have experienced.

God has not lost control. He is not a man that He should be nervous or concerned over any force that may be opposing you today. He still has all power in Heaven and earth. He knows the end from the beginning. And He will not let you fall.

I have discovered the most remarkable and exciting truth about God! Sometimes what appears to be a troubling and frightening event is actually the hand of God stirring up our nest to bring us into the high place we have been desiring. Really, it is! You see, like everybody else, sometimes we have a tendency to get comfortable and just sit down. Now, there's nothing wrong with resting and recuperating when we've gone through a time of challenge and labor. I believe God expects us to use wisdom in caring for our bodies and our minds.

But sometimes, long after we're rested and fit, we keep on sitting back with our feet up and watching the world go by. When that happens, our nest is likely to get stirred until we find ourselves pushed back into the mainstream of life.

Every time that happens to me, I find encouragement in the example of how the mother eagle takes care of her young. It's one of the most beautiful stories in all of nature. In the Bible, the mother eagle is likened to God himself. And when you study her ways, you realize what a beautiful portrayal this is of the Father.

In preparation for the birth of her offspring, the mother eagle builds a nest high in the mountains. She forms it with twigs, lines it with briars, then covers them with bits of fur and soft, downy feathers plucked from her own breast.

When the little eagles burst into the world, they have it made—food, security, comfort, and serenity. Life is beautiful. The mother's presence is reassuring, loving, powerful. And they grow in peace.

Then, after several weeks of bliss, the mother eagle begins stirring the nest with her sharp talons, digging out of the soft feathers and fur, exposing the briars and leaving the bewildered eaglets in a state of shock!

They begin to squirm and flutter, trying to escape the sharp briars and somehow find refuge from this horrible nightmare thrust upon them.

But no matter how they struggle to get comfortable again, the nest is now a place of suffering. Suddenly the mother eagle rises above them, unfolds her wings and arches them as if to say, "Don't worry. I am watching over you. Everything's in control."

Placing the tip of one great wing on the rim of the nest, she encourages her little ones to get off the briars and on the wing. Confused by her strange actions, the eaglets hesitate, wondering what to do next. Then, having no other choice, they wobble out onto their mother's great wingspread.

WHHOOOSSHHH!! She takes off and begins to soar, her little ones holding on for dear life. They are paralyzed with fear, and yet they are exhilarated by what is happening. They've never seen this dimension of life before, soaring above the clouds and riding the jet streams with such majesty. They begin to relax and enjoy the ride.

When the eagle returns them to the nest and covers the briars again, they are still reluctant to go back, looking forward to the next adventure.

After a few flights, one day they are gliding about at a high altitude, when the mother does another unexpected thing. She suddenly drops her wing, and throws the little eaglets into mid-air. They begin falling, heading for certain death on the jagged cliffs below! Tumbling helplessly end over end, the little balls of feathers screech frantically for help. But it looks like the end.

Then, with God-given precision, the mother eagle dives straight down, swoops under her little ones and catches them on her wing ... just in time to rescue them!

She repeats the process again ... then repeats it until her little ones reach out with their frail little wings one day and discover they are able to grab hold of the wind. Suddenly, they are buoyant ... flying on their own!

Perhaps they even realize that their mother had a purpose in what she was doing to them all along. But before they go out on their own, the mother eagle has one more lesson to teach her young. Sensing an approaching storm, she takes the young eagles aloft and shows them by example how to position themselves high in the mountains and set their wings so that the force of the storm causes them to rise above it. Together they ride it out, safe above the turbulence. Thus she teaches her little ones how to set their wings for the storms of life.

The apostle Paul learned this secret and developed the ability to live above the circumstances and storms of life. He gives his testimony in **Philippians 4:11-13**: *"Do not think that I am saying this under pressure of want. For I, however I am placed, have learnt to be independent of circumstances. I know how to face humble circumstances, and I know how to face prosperity. Into all and every human experience I have been initiated—into plenty and hunger, into prosperity and want. I can do everything in the strength of him who makes me strong"* (20th Century New Testament, emphasis added).

When Paul wrote the Philippian letter, he was in prison. Yet this epistle is often called the "Joy Letter" because there is such a spirit of optimism and victory in it. He did not let the circumstance of imprisonment rob him of his joy in the Lord.

You may be wondering why certain things are happening to you, why you've been hit with overwhelming losses and disappointments. Jesus provides the answer in John 10:10—*"The thief does not come except to steal, and to kill, and* to destroy. I have come that they might have life, and that they may have it more abundantly." The enemy may try to come against you. But remember, like the mother eagle, God undoubtedly is preparing you for something greater. Be sensitive to God's Holy Spirit. Be willing for *El Shaddai*—the God of more than enough—to stir your nest for a higher purpose. God uses these experiences to bring you into maturity.

The very tears that burned on your cheeks will begin to minister in their quiet but powerful way ... to bring inner healing. Many times God allows this built-in eyewash to bring things back into focus and help you to see His perfect will.

Consider the pearl and how it is formed. It begins as a grain of sand, an irritant that gets inside an oyster. When this happens, the oyster wraps the most precious part of its being around the foreign object ... layer upon layer it covers the irritation with a protecting, smoothing, healing substance. In time a pearl is produced, one of the most precious gems in all the world.

How do you handle the irritants that suddenly enter your life causing *discomfort* and *dis-ease*? The same way. Wrap the most precious part of yourself, your own faith in God, around your problem ... and watch God work!

God wants to do a great thing in your life. If you are harboring any negative thoughts and inner hurts, He wants you to throw open the windows of your inner being and allow the fresh breeze of the Holy Spirit to air out anything that might be festering or becoming stagnant.

Life is a fascinating experience ... a miracle force that courses through our bodies. It makes us aware of a moving Presence that somehow is not our own, but is given to us for a time.

more than enough for your circumstances

It is ever moving ... changing ... renewing itself within these temples of clay.

Sometimes traumatic experiences cause us to want to park away from the mainstream of life and give up. But life doesn't operate that way.

It doesn't matter whether you are facing the flush of life or a sudden disappointment, sickness or healing, mountaintop or valley ... every milestone of life has this sign written in blazing letters—"DON'T PARK HERE!"

Let me tell you, when the TV station we had planned to use as a production facility for our new TV ministry backed out of our agreement two weeks before we were to go on the air, I was troubled. I couldn't help wondering how God was going to work this new problem out.

You'd think after my years of involvement in faith ministry, I'd have learned that God is always true to His Word. But the old nature has the tendency to rise and try to interject fear and doubt about the things you are believing God for. On this occasion, the human side of me said, "Now what are you going to do? You've told everybody that God has given you a vision for reaching America through TV. And here it is a few weeks from the launching of your new program and you don't even have a TV studio to use!"

But then God's Word began to come alive in my heart. That's why it's so important to soak your spirit in His Word every day. When Satan comes against you, that stored reserve of energy will see you through.

Scripture verses began pouring into my consciousness ...

> "Be strong and of good courage, do not fear nor be afraid of them; for the Lord your God, He is the One who goes with you. He will not leave you nor forsake you" (Deuteronomy 31:6).

"But seek first the kingdom of God and His righteousness, and all these things shall be added to you" (Matthew 6:33).

"For assuredly, I say to you, whoever says to this mountain, 'Be removed and be cast into the sea,' and does not doubt in his heart, but believes that those things he says will come to pass, he will have whatever he says. Therefore I say to you, whatever things you ask when you pray, believe that you receive them, and you will have them" (Mark 11:23, 24).

"For with God nothing will be impossible" (Luke 1:37).

Trust in the Lord with all your heart, and lean not on your own understanding; in all your ways acknowledge Him, and He shall direct your paths (Proverbs 3:5, 6).

Who was I to question *El Shaddai*? After all, I had followed David's advice in Psalm 37:5 … *Commit your way to the Lord, trust also in Him, and He shall bring it to pass*—and if God is not a man that He should lie, then He would bring it to pass.

Sure enough, He did. The new daily TV program went on the air! It wasn't in as fancy a facility as I would have chosen, and things didn't go as smoothly as I would have liked them to go. But God accomplished what He said He would do—and in the process taught us some valuable lessons on trusting Him as our Source.

So don't be disheartened if a door closes in your face. When God opens a door for you, no man can shut it.

Don't be downhearted when the road to your goal seems to end. If your objective is in line with God's will, He simply has a detour planned that will give you an extra opportunity to grow in more productive ways that will be far more pleasing to you than the path you had originally chosen.

Instead of being disappointed, learn to be sensitive. Proverbs 16:9 says, *A man's heart plans his way, but the Lord directs his steps.*

A pastor friend of mine and his wife took some time off and traveled out of town for a much-needed time of rest and meditation. A friend had loaned them a beautiful motor home and they planned to just get away for a few days to seek God's direction for their large and growing church.

On the way they stopped at a shopping center, and while the pastor was waiting for his wife, an elderly couple pulled up beside the motor home, got out of their car and walked over to the vehicle.

"How do you like your motor home?" the man asked. My friend explained that it was just borrowed, but so far they were certainly enjoying it. The man explained his interest: "My wife and I have just retired, and we're thinking about buying one and traveling across the country."

So my pastor friend invited the couple to come in and take a look around. After they had seen the interior, they just kept standing around making small talk.

"By this time, my wife had come back, and we were eager to get on down the road," my friend said. "But the couple just kept on talking about the weather and many other things that really didn't seem too important."

Time dragged on, and the pastor and his wife, not wanting to be rude, began to feel a little frustrated.

"We both knew our time was limited," he said, "and we had our plans all made."

Finally, after the conversation had gone on for some time, a light clicked on in the minister's spirit. "Are you born again?" he asked the man.

"No," the visitor replied, "but my wife and I were just talking this morning about trying to find somebody to tell us how."

Thank God for men and women who are patient and sensitive to the Holy Spirit! "They just about had to beg us to tell them how to be saved," my friend laughed. "I think God would have kept us there all day until we realized what He wanted to see accomplished."

Today you may be facing a setback in your plans—but don't give up. If you're living for God and walking in faith, the Bible says that His plans will be accomplished in your life. Romans 8:28 makes that clear: *And we know that all things work together for good to those who love God, to those who are the called according to His purpose.*

El Shaddai—the God of more than enough—is working to achieve the very best for your life—and for the expansion and preservation of His kingdom.

When Daniel was thrown into the lions' den, he could have allowed himself to get more than a little upset. After all, that was not what he had planned for the day! But God was to use this situation for His glory, and no harm befell Daniel. His faith in God was continually exhibited. Yes, Daniel had his problems, but his solution was his unitedness in being a "doer" of the Word. He refused to give up his fellowship and trust in God.

When the three Hebrew children were placed in the fiery furnace, they could have questioned God's plan for them. But they kept on trusting Him. God wrapped them in the asbestos of His love so that when they came out of the furnace their clothes didn't even smell like smoke!

more than enough for your circumstances

Yes, there will be times of difficulty and great tests in your life. But the strength of *El Shaddai* will sustain you so that it will never be more than you can bear—and He will always provide a way out.

Paul faced persecution, beatings, imprisonment, hunger, thirst, and many other situations that could have brought defeat and disappointment. But he understood God's greater purpose. He declared, *But I want you to know brethren, that the things which happened to me have actually turned out for the furtherance of the gospel* (Philippians 1:12).

Paul understood, too, the laws of cause and effect, of sowing and reaping. He didn't blame God for his problems. He remembered his past—that he had led the persecution against the church at Jerusalem, and was part of the stoning of Stephen, the first Christian martyr. The Bible account also says, *"But Paul shamefully treated and laid waste the church continuously—with cruelty and violence; and entering house after house, he dragged out men and women and committed them to prison"* (Acts 8:3, Amplified Bible).

This is the way he had lived … and this is exactly what followed him every place he went. Don't misunderstand me—Paul was forgiven for the mistakes and the sin of his past. The wounds were healed—but the scars remained. Some of the seeds he sowed before his conversion still produced a bitter crop.

I'm told that attorneys sometimes make inadmissible statements in the courtroom, knowing that the opposing attorney will object. But even if the judge sustains the objections and instructs the jury to disregard the offending statement—the damage is already done! The idea has been planted in the minds of the jury members … a seed that will grow as they deliberate on the verdict.

So Paul faced adversity. No doubt many of his plans and dreams were never fulfilled. Imagine the force and the fury of the principalities and powers of evil that must have come against a man of his brilliance and dedication, a man given wholly to the divine call upon his life.

But did he complain or feel sorry for himself? Did he become bitter and ineffective because of the unpleasant circumstances he often faced? No, indeed. At the end of his life he could look back and say, "I want you to know that the things which have happened to me have actually turned out for the furtherance of the gospel."

So don't be disappointed when things don't seem to go your way. God is perfecting something better. He may have an assignment for you that's far beyond your greatest dreams. He's just waiting for your faith to catch up with His expectations. *Now to Him who is able to do exceedingly abundantly above all that we ask or think, according to the power that works in us* (Ephesians 3:20).

No matter what your situation, be like Paul—*Rejoice in the Lord always. Again I will say, rejoice! Let your gentleness be known to all men. The Lord is at hand. Be anxious for nothing, but in everything by prayer and supplication, with thanksgiving, let your requests be made known to God; and the peace of God which surpasses all understanding, will guard your hearts and minds through Christ Jesus. Finally, brethren, whatever things are true, whatever things are noble, whatever things are just, whatever things are pure, whatever things are lovely, whatever things are of good report, if there is any virtue and if there is anything praiseworthy—meditate on these things. The things which you learned and received and heard and saw in me, these do, and the God of peace will be with you* (Philippians 4:4-9). The rejoicing is in faith, believing in God's goodness.

more than enough for your circumstances

Let Hebrews 10:23 be your byword! *Let us hold fast the confession of our hope without wavering, for He who promised is faithful.*

And above all, strive to be patient before the Lord. *For you have need of endurance, so that after you have done the will of God, you may receive the promise ..." Now the just shall live by faith"* (Hebrews 10:36, 38).

El Shaddai—the God of more than enough—has great things waiting for you. And until you see them manifested, go before Him every day with this prayer:

Pray with me—

Father, how grateful I am that You have not lost control! It seems my world has gone crazy, yet I know that I know—it hasn't. You, Beloved, whisper tenderly to me Your personal involvement in all of life. We shall never be separated, eternally. Lord, I will grow. You didn't cause my problems, but You allow me to grow into the beautiful child who will bear Your mark of assurance to all who touch my life. Forgive me for saying You brought these hurtful life experiences into my path. I realize You are only good. I also confess I am independent of circumstances as Paul was, for the Greater One is in me. I trust in You with all of my heart and lean not on my own understanding, knowing You are now directing my path. Lord, You are directing my steps. In Jesus' Name, Amen.

chapter nine

more than enough for your every need

WHAT IS YOUR GREATEST NEED today? If I haven't talked about it yet in the pages of this book, let me assure you *El Shaddai* can still take care of it. He's more than enough for every need, every challenge, every mountain you may be facing. God is interested in everything that touches your life—if it concerns you, He cares.

Besides the thousands of promises that deal in detail with specific needs and clearly defined situations, God's Word also has many unlimited promises that cover a wide range of needs and desires. It's almost as if God said, "I'll take care of this and this and this … and if there's anything I didn't mention, I'll take care of it too."

One of my favorite "blank-check" promises is—*"If you abide in Me, and My words abide in you, you will ask what you desire, and it shall be done for you"* (**John 15:7**).

more than enough

I especially like Mrs. Reedy's translation of this verse: *"If you abide in me and my words have their place in you, you will pray to the Father and he will create or give birth to the things. He will make it come to pass."*

Isn't that tremendous? If what you need isn't in stock—even if it doesn't exist—God will create the thing you need and cause your desired situation to come to pass. Don't you just love the way *El Shaddai*—the God of more than enough—takes care of us? He will do it by His creative, miraculous power.

For the widow who gave the prophet Elijah her last bit of food and oil, God kept meal in her barrel for 1,300 days—and He put an oil well in her kitchen! The supply may not have *looked* abundant, but it never ran out—there was always more than enough.

For the children of Israel, trapped at the edge of the Red Sea, the Lord parted the waters so the people could walk across on dry land. The pursuing Egyptian army was destroyed, and Moses led the Israelites on into the wilderness, where God fed them and took care of their every need.

In New Testament times, when it looked like the wedding feast at Cana was ruined, Jesus, continuing to reveal the *El Shaddai* nature of God, turned water into wine. It was the best wine that was served that night—and there was plenty of the best!

When five thousand men plus their wives and children were hungry after listening to Jesus teach all day, He miraculously multiplied five loaves of bread and two fishes to provide food for the multitude. Everyone was satisfied, and there were twelve baskets of bread and fish left over. That's abundance. That's divine surplus. *El Shaddai* is the same in every age. He's more than enough!

Contrary to some people's thinking, the abundant blessings of *El Shaddai* go far beyond the absolute needs and necessities of life. As children of God, we need not settle for a minimum survival—we can enjoy God's best. That means we can ask God for some of the things we want. We don't absolutely have to have them, but we desire them. And God will give them to us.

You say, "Does the Bible teach this, Vicki?" Absolutely. Take a look at these thrilling verses from God's Word.

> *Trust in the Lord, and do good; dwell in the land, and feed on His faithfulness. Delight yourself also in the Lord, and He shall give you the desires of your heart. Commit your way to the Lord, trust also in Him, and He shall bring it to pass* (Psalm 37:3-5).

Do you see it? Trust in the Lord and He'll feed you. Delight yourself in the Lord and He'll give you the desires of your heat. Commit your way unto Him and He'll bring it to pass. What an exciting series of promises. And I can tell you from personal experience that they really work.

Shortly after we moved to Tulsa, Mother and I decided we'd like to have a dog. Not just any dog—he had to have certain definite traits and qualities. We didn't care what breed the dog was, but he had to be "just right" for us.

I said, "Lord, send us a dog that is completely trained and housebroken. He must not get on the furniture. He must be bright and intelligent, and he must adore Mother and me."

In the busy days that followed when we were getting settled into the house and working hard to launch the new television program, I didn't mention a dog again. Mother thought I had forgotten about it, but I really hadn't. She was so eager to have a pet that she wanted to go out to the dog pound and look for one.

I was specific with God. I reminded Him of the dog and how I preferred to have Him find a pet for us.

One morning two or three days later, I picked up my briefcase and started for the office. Just as I walked by the breakfast room window, I saw a beautiful silver schnauzer run by. Something inside told me this was my dog. So I ran over and caught him.

He was so well-behaved and well-groomed I felt sure he had just wandered away from home. Phil and Fern Halverson, who have worked with me in the ministry, were staying at the house with Mother and me, and Phil went with me around the neighborhood to see if we could find the dog's owner. As we looked, we saw another lady out walking her dog. She said she had been all through the neighborhood many times and knew of only two houses where the dog might belong.

We checked with the people at those houses, and he didn't belong to them. We checked with the animal shelter, newspaper personal ads, shopping center bulletin boards—no one knew anything about the dog. So we kept him, and Mother named him Pete!

Well, let me tell you, Pete has become a member of our family. He's perfectly trained, and never even tries to get on the furniture. Pete is the sharpest, most intelligent, most outstanding animal I've ever seen. He responds perfectly to voice commands, and you only have to tell him one time. And, of course, he just loves us so much!

God gave us the desire of our hearts—in this case, a beautiful dog.

I'm sure you noticed that the promises in Psalm 37 all have conditions—things to do to qualify for the blessing. Trust ... delight yourself ... commit your

more than enough for your every need

way. <mark>This is the way God deals with His people, in covenants.</mark> A covenant is an agreement, a contract. God says, "You do this, then I'll do that." And the covenant always works in our favor. Usually our part of the bargain involves trusting God and obeying His divine laws. That puts us in position to receive everything we need for an abundant life.

Miracles are waiting for you! But if you'll go back and study the many miracles in the Bible, you'll see that they invariably followed an act of obedience and/or faith. ☆

Samson had to reach out in his weakness and grab hold of the pillars of the temple of the Philistines before God gave him the strength to pull them down.

Moses, at Horeb, had to obey God and hit a dry rock with a dusty stick before *El Shaddai* caused an abundance of cool, clear water to burst forth in the parched desert.

And Elijah had to go and sit at the brook of Cherith as God commanded before *El Shaddai* caused an abundance of cool, clear water to burst forth in the parched desert.

The truth is repeated over and over—"*if you are willing and obedient, you shall eat the good of the land*" (Isaiah 1:19).

Those who seek the Lord shall not lack any good thing (Psalm 34:10).

"*But seek first the kingdom of God and His righteousness, and all these things shall be added to you*" (Matthew 6:33).

Abundance should be a way of life for the believer. As a child of God, you are a joint-heir with Jesus. And He possesses all things.

God doesn't know about deficit spending. He's not on budget. His resources are unlimited, and everything He has is available to His children.

He who did not spare His own Son, but delivered Him up for us all, how shall He not with Him also freely give us ALL things? (Romans 8:32).

Second Peter 1:3 confirms that fact. *As His divine power has given to us all things that pertain to life and godliness, through the knowledge of Him who called us by glory and virtue.*

Latch onto that important word—"ALL." It's nestled in the middle of so many promises ... *Who forgives ALL your iniquities, who heals ALL your diseases* (Psalm 103:3).

And my God shall supply ALL your need according to His riches in glory by Christ Jesus (Philippines 4:19).

"ALL authority has been given to Me in heaven and on earth" (Matthew 28:18).

Obedience brings abundance

El Shaddai is eager to work miracles in our lives as we conform ourselves to the expressed will of the Father. Obedience brings abundance. Labor brings blessings. Perseverance brings results.

Don't be afraid of the concept of obedience. It should not carry a negative connotation of getting down under some oppressive power. Obedience is actually an opportunity God affords you to follow His leadership into the higher ways for your life. Its purpose is to bring you to the wonderful place you've desired to reach but didn't know how to get to on your own. Obedience is a

more than enough for your every need

positive guideline to goodness! It is cooperating with the Holy Spirit. You see, God is not wanting you to buckle under to obey. Instead, He wants to help you overcome your old habits and patterns and discover the fullness of His positive, productive plan for your life.

The secret is to do what you can do to the best of your ability, and turn the rest over to Jesus. When He tells you what to do—do it with all your heart. When he says stop, don't move a muscle! Just walk by faith—do what the Lord leads you to do.

Satan may come against you and try to make you feel foolish. But if you'll keep on obeying God, you'll see the manifestation of His promise. He never goes back on His Word.

I learned a long time ago that good things are worth waiting for. And the longer you serve Him, the more you'll realize that He always fulfills His Word at exactly the right time at the right place and in the right way.

Let 2 Corinthians 9:8 be your watchword: *God is able to make all grace abound toward you, that you, always having all sufficiency in all things, have an abundance for every good work.*

Put God to the test. Tell Him what you need or desire. Ask Him what He would have you to do. Then do it. And you will discover that *El Shaddai*—the God of more than enough—is able (and eager) to meet your every need.

Now let's pray—

Provider, Father, Your divine Words are abiding in me, and as I pray them they shall become containers of power. Your Word shall not return to You void but full of power. I am learning to delight myself in You, Lord, and to commit my way to You … and You bring to pass the things that I need. I am seeking Your Kingdom and righteousness, knowing that all things are being added unto me. You are able to make all grace abound toward me, that I, always having all sufficiency in all things, have an abundance for every good work. In Jesus' Name, Amen.

chapter ten

releasing the power of El Shaddai

IT'S ONE THING TO BE aware of the unlimited resources of *El Shaddai*—the God of more than enough—and another thing entirely to take full advantage of the resources the Almighty One wants you to have.

In this book, we've looked at many specific areas of life in which His power may be felt in your life. We've proven from the Word of God that His will for your life and mine is to be totally victorious over all the power of the enemy. But even knowing what the Bible says about the power of God is not enough. Such knowledge is useless if it is not put into practical application.

In the beginning of the early church, the first Christian believers spent much time in fasting and prayer. They were drinking in the power of the Holy Spirit and building themselves up, waiting before the Lord. But there came a time when the Holy Spirit said, *"Now separate to Me Barnabas and Saul for the work to which I have called them"* (Acts 13:2).

What would have happened if they had kept on fasting, kept on praying, kept on waiting before the Lord?

Nothing. The first missionary evangelistic team would not have gone forth. The revival would not have begun. The work Barnabas and Saul were called to do would never have started.

You see, there is a time to pray ... and a time to obey. There is a time to act.

Oh, sure. I know there are some people who are eager to act before they know God's will, before they study His Word, before they pray and wait before the Lord. And I would be the first to agree that acting in that manner almost always leads to failure.

But it's also possible to pray too much about a situation. There's no use to keep on praying when God has spoken and told you what to do. Then it's time to get moving. Because the fullness of God's power is not released without action.

What kind of action? What God has told you to do.

How will He tell You? In various ways—through His Word, through the voices of His prophets, through revelation by the Holy Spirit, through that still, small voice that causes you to know that you know that you know.

I believe in intercessory prayer.

I believe in waiting before the Lord.

I believe in studying God's precious Holy Word.

But I also believe that the power of *El Shaddai*, the Almighty One, can only be released by taking action ... by obeying God and doing what He has commanded. I believe in obeying God. That is the key to releasing the power of *El Shaddai*.

Let me share with you how my ministry began—how I released God's power into my life. You see, I knew about the power of God—I believed in it. I knew what the Word of God taught—the principles and precepts of the Bible were clear and plain in my understanding. I knew how to pray—to communicate personally, one to one, with my heavenly Father. And I knew the Lord's will for my life—that He had called me to the ministry.

But I was resisting I didn't want to go into the ministry. I was running away from the call of God.

Actually, it was a bit difficult to run because I was gravely ill. By this time in my spiritual growth, my faith was developed to the point that I could release God's healing power into my life. But I had a serious physical ailment that was not being healed.

God didn't make me sick. He didn't afflict my body with this ailment or condition. But my being out of the flow of His Spirit—out of harmony with His highest and best will for me—blocked my healing.

I wasn't walking in faith.

I wasn't walking in the direction God was leading.

I wasn't answering His call for my life.

So I reached the point where it was necessary to go ahead and have surgery. A week later blood clots hit my lungs. For the next two months I was in and out of Methodist Hospital in Dallas.

During that period I didn't pray to get well. In fact, I really didn't talk to God at all. Oh, I loved Him, but I was embarrassed to think that I was supposed to be a person of such great faith—yet I'd had this colossal faith failure.

Do you know what God did to me during this time? He just loved me! He saw that everything I needed was provided. The abiding, restful, nurturing presence of *El Shaddai* just hung around me. He didn't rebuke me, reprove me, or convict me. He just loved me with a deep, abiding love that surrounded and uplifted and warmed me through and through.

God waited until I was ready to talk. Never once did He try to force a confrontation until I was ready. And that time came. During the second month of this experience, I awoke at five o'clock one morning to hear the gentle voice of the Lord asking me three questions:

Will you go where I want you to go?

Will you do what I want you to do?

Will you be what I want you to be?

I listened ... and I said, "Yes, Lord—yes!"

From that moment I began to recover. God and I knew that we had settled some divine business. And the release I felt allowed me to receive complete healing.

It didn't happen in an instant. It didn't happen in a day, or even a week. But in a very short time the killing condition doctors couldn't effectively treat was defeated and I was more alive than I'd ever been in my whole life. I was still a bit weak at times—but I could feel divine strength pulsing and surging through me.

Two months after I got out of the hospital, I was asked to speak at a ladies' luncheon at a Full Gospel Businessmen's convention in Dallas. I couldn't wait to get there. I knew it was going to be the beginning—the time when God's power was released in my life. When they announced I would be speaking at the luncheon in the evening service the night before, I felt like standing up and shouting, "It's going to be the greatest miracle service you've ever seen!"

So I went to the meeting the next day. About five hundred ladies were there. I thanked them for praying for me that I would live. I explained how I had learned so much from my sickness, and actually made my decision to enter the ministry while I was ill.

Then the Holy Spirit directed me to make a specific statement. It puzzled me at first, but I repeated word for word what the Spirit told me to say—"Don't blame God for what happened to me!"

The instant I said that, I saw a soft, billowy cloud drop through the ceiling and into the room. I looked up and to the left and there was a cloud—inside the hotel!

So I said it again—"Don't blame God for what happened to me!" And the cloud dropped even lower. I saw it. It was as real to me as the paper and ink you are holding in your hand. And the presence of the Lord was so real and vivid that every person in the room was aware of it.

I didn't say any more—there was no need to go on. I simply asked that everyone who wanted to know Jesus, who wanted to be filled with the Spirit, who wanted to be healed, to come to the front.

Women jumped up and ran to the front. I don't mean they just moved quickly. They literally jumped up and ran. I've never seen anything like it. They lined up two and three deep across the front of the auditorium. I went down to minister to them. When I raised my hand to touch the first lady—I remember she had beautiful red hair—before I could touch her she fell under the power of God.

I was amazed. I instinctively made a sweeping gesture with my hand and everywhere I pointed women fell to the floor. The air was so charged with the electric presence of *El Shaddai* that I could hardly breathe.

Suddenly a surge of God's power rushed through me and I went down. My mother and another woman were behind me, and they pulled me up and half carried me all over that auditorium. They just sort of aimed me and pushed! Wherever I went I recognized what the ladies were being healed of, and when I reached out to touch them they would fall. I went all over the ballroom, leaving a trail of bodies on the floor. There must have been nearly 200 women who fell under God's power.

The waiters and waitresses came to see what was happening. When they walked in, the power of God swept across the room and several of them fell down.

The men of the convention heard the commotion and came to see what was going on. As they walked into the room, they fell.

When I walked out of the auditorium to get on the elevator, everyone I passed fell under the power of God. I felt that I was dangerous! I thought I could never be out in public again.

Later I was to learn that, through the Holy Spirit, the manifestation of God's power can be channeled and directed—that He is never out of control. God's power is like a laser beam that has raw power enough to slice through steel beams like butter and yet may be so precisely directed that it can be used in eye surgery to remove cataracts.

But *El Shaddai*—the God of more than enough—knew what was needed on that occasion. He knew the only way He could convince me and everyone around me that He actually had called me was to demonstrate His power through me in a spectacular, unlimited display. I'll never forget it as long as I live.

It was a lavish setting, in a ballroom with beautiful chandeliers, tables with beautiful tablecloths—everything refined and elegant. In that setting, *El Shaddai* came and showed Himself in all His splendor and glory. He focused attention on Himself to let people see just a small measure of His unlimited power to bless mankind.

Since that day my life has never been the same. Every day I have felt the power of *El Shaddai* flowing through me as I have ministered to others. I have learned to keep releasing His power and opening myself to be a channel of blessing.

You can release that power in your life as well. And if you've ever felt like crying out, "Don't just tell me to do it, TELL ME HOW"—this chapter is for you. In it I've outlined and explained eight steps, or keys, you can use to release the power of *El Shaddai*. You may know most of them—you may already be using them in principle. But if you ever feel weak and helpless—if the promises of God just don't seem to be working for you—read this chapter again and check yourself to see if you've forgotten to follow the biblical pattern ... the guidelines for scriptural success.

Remember, *El Shaddai*—the God of more than enough—is ready and willing to release His power and provide every need in your life. In fact, the

Word says that He delights in your prosperity. *"Let the Lord be magnified, who has pleasure in the prosperity of His servant"* (Psalm 35:27).

And 3 John 2 should be familiar to every believer. *"Beloved, I pray that you may prosper in all things and be in health, just as your soul prospers."*

Yes, *El Shaddai* wants to make you successful. But He requires that you do things His way … that you live according to His statutes.

Isaiah 48:17 says, *"I am the Lord your God who teaches you to profit, who leads you by the way you should go."*

1. **Believe the abundant life is God's will for you**

The first key to unlocking the blessings of *El Shaddai* is to believe that it is His will for you to enjoy His abundance. Jesus made that clear when He said, *"The thief does not come except to steal, and to kill, and to destroy. I have come that they may have life, and that they may have it more abundantly"* (John 10:10).

God wants you to prosper. His Word is His will, and it contains more than 7,000 promises for your well-being and spiritual abundance.

So when you pray concerning needs in your life, pray with thanksgiving … with boldness … with assurance. Your needs are met when you trust Him without wavering, knowing that what His Word promises is yours.

2. **Discover the work God has called you to do**

The second key to walking with power is to actively seek out the life-work for which you are best suited. If it is still not clear to you what God would have you do with your life, pray until He reveals that to you.

Discontentment is a favorite tool of the enemy. Thousands of people are in careers that are less than God's perfect will. They are bound to their jobs by financial necessity, or a need for recognition, or family tradition. Your grandfather was a dentist; your father was a dentist—so naturally, you should want to be a dentist, too. No! Have the courage to be what you feel God wants you to be.

Conversely, many people are unhappy in their life-work—even though they are doing what God wants them to do. We forget that God distributes gifts to His children severally as He will. Some people are ideally suited to be accountants—but they desire to be evangelists. Others are best suited for sales or industrial work—but long to be prophets.

Learn to be content in the place God has created for you—but always be sensitive to His direction. Remember, Jesus leads—Satan pushes. Jesus asks—the devil compels.

Ask God to lead you into the life-work He would have you to do. When He makes that clear to you, then do all you can to succeed in that profession. When you've done all that's possible, *El Shaddai* will take care of the impossible. He will always be more than enough for your shortcomings.

3. Have faith in God

The third key to superabundance is a strong faith in God. Believing is the first step—but faith puts wheels on your belief.

Someone has said that hope is the grabhook by which you latch onto your dreams. Faith is the rope attached to the grabhook.

First, you catch a vision of God's power and abundance. Then, you set your hopes on attaining it. Faith is the way you get there.

God is an immovable rock. He will never fail. But our hopes and our faith fluctuate. The key to achieving God's best is to develop our faith to rock-hard consistency.

The day you really understand that God will always be there, that He will never let you down if you come to Him in faith, according to His Word, is the first day of a life filled with unlimited resources and spiritual blessings.

No matter how big the obstacle you may encounter, you can move it through the power of *El Shaddai*.

The secret is to cast your cares at His feet. Turn the controls of your life over to Him. He can see farther than you can see. He can work out things that are invisible to you.

Stand today on Psalm 127:2, and you'll never have to worry again. *It is vain for you to rise up early, to take rest late, to eat the bread of [anxious] toil; for he gives [blessings] to his beloved in sleep (Amplified Bible).*

Tonight, you can close your eyes and enjoy a good night's sleep—*El Shaddai* is watching over you!

4. Establish a partnership with God

The fourth key to superabundance is to establish a covenant or partnership with God. Make Him your Executive Officer and realize that He has given you the power of attorney to carry on His business in this world.

With that divine authority, or *exousia*, comes a reward in kingdom benefits. You see, being involved in the Father's business offers more than a great retirement plan. There are some fantastic fringe benefits!

To start with, there is unlimited health insurance. Read your contract, or covenant, and you'll see that His stated policy includes divine health.

Look at the health clause in Proverbs 4:20-22: *My son, give attention to my words; incline your ear to my sayings. Do not let them depart from your eyes; keep them in the midst of your heart; for they are life to those who find them, and health to all their flesh.*

Not only is your health insurance provided, but God's company offers a great profit sharing program that pays dividends while you are working. Check the employee stockholder's section in Mark 10:29, 30—*So Jesus answered and said, "Assuredly, I say to you, there is not one who has left house or brothers or sisters or father or mother or wife or children or lands, for My sake and the gospel's, who shall not receive a hundredfold now in this time."*

Follow His counsel. Be faithful to perform every task He gives you to do. When you adhere to His corporate guidelines (His Word)—willingly and obediently—there is no limit to your advancement potential.

5. **Be bold to launch out in new ventures**

The fifth step in releasing the power of *El Shaddai* is to be unafraid in launching out into new ventures. If you have been praying for things to happen, get ready to act. Expect some exciting changes and challenges.

When God says to move, step out in faith. Don't limit Him by your own evaluation of yourself. Even if you doubt your own ability, if God says you can do it—you can. Ask God to let you see yourself as He sees you.

When God told me to leave Dallas, move to Tulsa, and begin a daily television ministry, my natural reaction was to say, "You've got to be kidding." But I've learned to recognize His voice, and when He speaks, I act.

On the other hand, you need to be sure you're hearing the voice of God, not your own desires ... or even the voice of the enemy. There is a fine line that separates faith from presumption.

God will give you faith to believe for a tremendous amount of money, but He won't lead you to spend it before it comes. He will allow your ministry to expand beyond your wildest expectations, but He will do it by His own law of increase. Seeds don't produce a harvest overnight. And while eternity is not limited by the dimension of time, it is governed by a sequence of events.

It took God six days to create the world and all that's in it. So don't expect Him to give you everything at the snap of a finger. *"For you have need of steadfast patience and endurance, so that you may perform and fully accomplish the will of God, and thus receive and carry away [and enjoy to the full] what is promised"* (Hebrews 10:36, *Amplified Bible*).

6. Obey the Golden Rule

The sixth key to receiving from God is obeying the Golden Rule. Jesus never took advantage of another man to realize a profit. He always did unto others as He would have them to do unto Him. So God would not bless you to everyone else's hurt. *The blessing of the Lord makes one rich, and He adds no sorrow with it* (Proverbs 10:22). And that's the guideline He's given to every believer.

> *"Then the King will say to those on His right hand, 'Come, you blessed of My Father, inherit the kingdom prepared for you from the foundation of the world: for I was hungry and you gave Me food, I was thirsty and you gave Me drink, I was a stranger and you took Me in, I was naked and you clothed Me, I was sick and you came to Me. I was in prison and you came to Me.' Then the righteous will answer Him, saying, 'Lord, when did we see You hungry and feed You, or thirsty and give You drink? When did we see You a stranger and take You in, or naked and clothe You? Or when did we see You sick, or in prison, and come to You?' And the King will answer and say to them, 'Assuredly, I say to you, inasmuch as you did it to one of the least of these My brethren, you did it to Me"* (Matthew 25:34-40).

The Bible says that Jesus went about doing good. If you want to enjoy His benefits, go thou and do likewise!

7. Put God first

Step number seven is spelled out in Matthew 6:33—*"Seek first the kingdom of God and His righteousness, and all these things shall be added to you."*

Such a simple truth—but one that eludes so many people. Seek the kingdom of God ... seek His will for your life ... seek out every opportunity to give love and care to everyone you meet. When you do these things, then God will meet your needs.

That's a divine principle that applies in every area of life. We are to seek the Creator—not the creature ... the Giver—not the gifts ... the Holy Spirit—not outward manifestations. You see, signs and wonders FOLLOW those who believe. We are not to seek the blessings and manifestations of *El Shaddai*. But when we seek Him, His blessings will overtake us.

8. **Pay your tithes and put God to the test!**

The eighth and final step on the road to prosperity and spiritual power could well be the first. It's defined very succinctly in Proverbs 3:9, 10. *Honor the Lord with your possessions, and with the firstfruits of all your increase; so your barns will be filled with plenty, and your vats will overflow with new wine.*

That verse is talking about the rewards that come from paying your tithes—the first tenth of your income.

God promises in Malachi 3:10, 11, *"Bring all the tithes into the storehouse, that there may be food in My house, and prove Me now in this,"* says the Lord of hosts, *"If I will not open for you the windows of heaven and pour out for you such blessings that there will not be room enough to receive it. And I will rebuke the devourer for your sakes, so that he will not destroy the fruit of your ground, nor shall the vine fail to bear fruit for you in the field,"* says the Lord of hosts.

Now that's what I call prosperity—and it's yours if you'll just be faithful in giving God a tenth of everything that comes your way.

You see, it all belongs to Him. But He asks for only ten percent—and our willingness to let Him use everything He needs.

Don't be afraid to let God have your finances. When you let Him have everything you have, He gives you access to everything He has. His Word says, *"Give, and it will be given to you: good measure, pressed down, shaken together, and running over will be put into your bosom. For with the same measure that you use, it will be measured back to you"* (Luke 6:38).

If you expect to receive bountiful blessings, learn to give bountifully. Frances Hunter says that when you give to God with a teaspoon, He gives back to you with a teaspoon. But when you give to Him with a shovel, He gives back with a shovel—and His shovel is a lot bigger than yours!

The apostle Paul explains it this way: *He who sows sparingly will also reap sparingly, and he who sows bountifully will also reap bountifully. So let each one give as he purposes in his heart, not grudgingly or of necessity; for God loves a cheerful giver. And God is able to make all grace abound toward you, that you, always having all sufficiency in all things, have an abundance for every good work* (2 Corinthians 9:6-8).

Make tithing and giving a way of life for your family. Teach it to your children from the time they're old enough to understand.

When you live by faith—God's way—you release the power of *El Shaddai*. And no matter what your need might be, you'll always have more than enough!

And now, let's pray together—

Father, I will submit to You ... and I act on Your Word and the leading of Your Spirit in my life. Now I will do the things I have been afraid to do. I will become a thoughtful witness of Your goodness. I will become a loving person. I will give on every level—financially, lovingly, to each opportunity that is presented to me. I will take action in my life to totally follow You. I am aware that You desire that I prosper in all things and be in health as my soul is prospering. You teach me to profit and lead me by the way I should go. I magnify You, Lord. You have pleasure in the prosperity of Your servant. I trust You, rejoice in You and Your goodness. Your Word will not depart from my eyes, my ear is inclined to your sayings—they do not depart from my eyes and I am keeping them in the midst of my heart. They are life to me and health to my flesh. In Jesus' Name, Amen.

workbook

This workbook has been prepared to enhance
the teachings in the book,
More than Enough, Encountering El Shaddai

more than enough

chapter one
"I am El Shaddai"

Part 1. Please complete the following statements using the text as your guide.

1. The Hebrew word most often translated into English as "God" is __ELOHIM__. This name comes from words which mean __STRENGTH__, or the __STRONG__ one, and to swear or bind oneself by an oath, implying __FAITHFULNESS__.

2. The second primary name of God, translated as "Lord" is __JEHOVAH__, or the self-existent One, which means the eternal __I AM__, who reveals Himself.

3. The third primary Hebrew word for God is Adon or Adonai, meaning __MASTER__, or translated in English it is __LORD__.

4. Please complete the meanings of each of the following names of God

   a. Jehovah-jireh: the Lord who __PROVIDES__.

   b. Jehovah-rapha: the Lord who __HEALS__.

   c. Jehovah-nissi: the Lord our __BANNER__, symbol of __VICTORY__ in battle.

   d. Jehovah-shalom: the Lord our __PEACE__.

   e. Jehovah-ra-ah: the Lord my __SHEPHERD__.

   f. Jehovah-Tsidkenu: the Lord our __RIGHTEOUSNESS__.

   g. Jehovah-shammah: the Lord is __PRESENT__.

(These are the different attributes or characteristics of one true God.)

5. Of all the names of God, the most touching and meaningful to me is El Shaddai. "El" signifies the __STRONG ONE__. "Shaddai," from the Hebrew word, Shad, means __THE BREAST__.

6. God, as Shaddai, is:

   a. __THE NOURISHER__.

   b. __THE STRENGTH - GIVER__.

   c. __THE SATISFIER__ (who pours Himself into believing lives).

7. In God's presence (at His Breast) we receive __IMMUNITY__ against all hurtful forces that might attack and are __COMFORTED__ by the rhythm of the heart of God.

8. El Shaddai not only enriches; He also makes fruitful. The Lord said to Abram, "I am Almighty God—El Shaddai—I will multiply you exceedingly … I will make you exceedingly __FRUITFUL__" (Genesis 17:1, 2, 6).

9. Once we become productive, El Shaddai becomes a __CHASTENING PURIFYING__ force to make us even more fruitful.

10. The characteristic name of God—El Shaddai—appears __31__ times in the book of Job.

11. In the midst of Job's grief, hurt, and heartbreak, he __PRAISED__ God.

more than enough

12. Sometimes we need to shut ourselves away from outside influences and let God's presence pour through our inner being until we are running over with the REVELATION of His divine nature.

13. What you make happen for others, God will make happen for YOU .

Part 2. TRUE OR FALSE: Please put a T in the blank if the statement is True; F if the statement is False.

 T 1. Man is still in tremendous need of the strength and faithfulness of Elohim.

 T 2. Having a close association with people who are constantly negative, foul-mouthed, or malicious in their spirit can pull us down to destruction.

workbook

chapter two
"more than enough for your salvation"

Part 1. Please complete the following statements using the text as your guide.

1. Paul said, "One thing I do, _forgetting_ those things which are behind and reaching forward to those things which are ahead, I press toward the _mark_ for the prize of the _high calling_ of God in Christ Jesus. Therefore let us, as many as are mature, have this mind" (Philippians 3:13-15).

2. According to Lamentations 3:22-23, God's mercies are new _every morning_.

3. God's salvation is more than enough for our _SHEEP_ nature. He goes out and finds us and tenderly carries us back to the _PROTECTION_ of His fold.

4. El Shaddai—the God of more than enough—wants to deliver us from all guilt and condemnation. Guilt invariably produces _CONDEMNATION_.

5. John 3:17 says, "For God did not send His Son into the world to _CONDEMN_ the world, but that the world through Him might be _SAVED_."

6. One of the most destructive aspects of fear is _NEGATIVE_ thinking. _FAITH_ cannot exist with negative thinking.

7. The Greek words translated "salvation" actually speak of what four (4) things?

   a. __HEALTH__

   b. __DELIVERANCE__

   c. __SAFETY__

   d. __VICTORY__

8. If you draw near to God, He will __draw near__ to you (James 4:8).

9. God has more than enough love, mercy, and forgiveness to cleanse every __MISTAKE__ and give you a brand-new lease on life.

10. Romans 8:1-2 says, "There is therefore now no __condemnation__ to those who are in Christ Jesus, who do not walk according to the flesh, but according to the __Spirit__. For the law of the __Spirit of Life__ in Christ Jesus has made me free from the law of sin and death."

11. Acts 2:38 (Amplified) speaks of the forgiveness of and release from sins that are repented of. "Repent—change your views, and purpose to accept the will of God in your inner selves instead of rejecting it—and be baptized every one of you in the name of Jesus Christ for the __FORGIVENESS__ of and __RELEASE__ from your sins."

12. True repentance means "__CHANGING__ your views and thinking __DIFFERENTLY__."

workbook

13. The Apostle Paul described "repentance" by saying that men "should repent and turn to God and do __WORKS__ and __LIVE__ lives consistent with and __WORTHY__ of their repentance" (Acts 26:20, AMP.).

14. Romans 10:9-10 explains "how" to be saved. "If you __CONFESS__ with your mouth the Lord Jesus and __BELIEVE__ in your heart that God has raised Him from the dead, you will be saved. For with the heart one believes to righteousness, and with the mouth confession is made to salvation."

15. When you are born again, you are "in Christ" and you become a __NEW CREATION__ (2 Corinthians 5:17). When you are born again, God wipes your record clean and gives you a new start.

16. God originally planned for His relationship with man to be a warm, intimate, and personal friendship. Through Adam's sin, mankind was separated from full fellowship with God. __JESUS__ redeemed man from Satan's domination. When we accept Jesus' redemption, then our relationship with God is __RESTORED__ and you are given __DOMINION__ over all things.

17. A born-again believer is a __CHILD__ of God and a __JOINT HEIR__ with Jesus Christ (Romans 8:17).

18. When Jesus Christ lives in you, you can do all things God has ordained for you to do through His __POWER__ (Philippians 4:13; Acts 1:8).

Part 2. TRUE OR FALSE: Please put a T in the blank if the statement is True; F if the statement is False.

__T__ 1. God's grace is sufficient for any and all sin.

__T__ 2. God is more than enough for our salvation.

__T__ 3. To receive salvation means to be rescued and defended.

__T__ 4. God's children are to reign in life.

workbook

chapter three
"more than enough for your inner power"

Part 1. Please complete the following statements using the text as your guide.

1. Man was different from the rest of creation in that he was created in the _likeness_ and _image_ of God, and God breathed into his nostrils the _breath of life_ _____.

2. According to Dr. Roy Blizzard's studies of Hebrew texts, he said Genesis 2:7 actually reads: "And the Lord God Elohim created Adam from the minute particles of the _totality_ of all that God is."

3. Not only are we made in the image and likeness of God, but the divine life force of the Creator is actually within us—an _unlimited_ and _unconquerable_ inner power.

4. The Psalmist David said of God's creation, "What is man, that You are mindful of him, and the son of [earthborn] man, that You care for him? Yet You have made him but little lower than God [or heavenly beings], and You have crowned him with _glory_ and _honor_. You made him to have _dominion_ over the works of Your hands; You have put _all things_ under his feet" (Psalm 8:4-6 AMP.).

5. Believers sometimes feel weak and helpless when they focus on the outer world and respond to the wrong influences around them. They react with ___feelings___ and feelings can easily be manipulated by the enemy.

6. To be victorious over earthly adversity or negative spiritual forces, we must bring our ___inner___ power to bear on the problem. In other words, think on the ___El Shaddai___ force within you.

7. Isaiah gave four (4) promises for those who wait upon the Lord. Please name them (Isaiah 40:31).

   a. ___Renew our strength___
   b. ___Mount up w/ wings like eagles___
   c. ___Run and not grow weary___
   d. ___Walk and not faint___

8. ___Christ in us, the hope of glory___ causes inner power to overflow from deep inside us.

9. John said, "You are of God, little children, and have overcome … because He Who is in you is ___greater___ than he who is in the world" (1 John 4:4).

10. ___Visualizing___ releases an unseen but all-powerful faith force that directs all the strength and resources of El Shaddai to our assistance.

11. James said, "Count it all joy when you fall into various trials, knowing that the testing of your faith produces ___patience___. But let

patience have its perfect work, that you may be __perfect__ and __complete__, lacking nothing" (James 1:2-4).

12. The joy of the Lord is your __strength__ (Nehemiah 8:10).

13. When you accept Jesus Christ as your Lord and Savior, He gives you EXOUSIA or __divine authority__. He gives you the "power of attorney" to conduct the __Master's__ business.

14. The authority we are given as a born-again child of God is mentioned in Luke 10:19. "Behold, I give you the authority ... over __all__ the power of the enemy, and __nothing__ shall by any means hurt you."

15. This is the same authority Jesus gave to the twelve disciples in Luke 9:1. "Then He called His twelve disciples together and gave them _____ __power__ and __authority__ over all demons, and to cure diseases."

16. When you minister in the power of the Holy Spirit, Jesus gives you __dunamis__, or miracle-working power, as spoken of in Acts 1:8. "But you shall receive __power__ when the Holy Spirit has come upon you."

17. Jesus was anointed with this same dunamis power. "God anointed Jesus of Nazareth with the Holy Spirit and with __power__, who went about doing good and healing all who were oppressed by the devil, for God was with Him" (Acts 10:38).

18. As you grow in faith, you develop kratos, the kind of strength described in Ephesians 6:10. "Finally, my brethren, be strong in the Lord and in the _____power_____ of His might."

19. Paul said in 2 Corinthians 2:14 that God always leads us in _____triumph_____.

Part 2. TRUE OR FALSE: Please put a T in the blank if the statement is True; F if the statement is False.

__T__ 1. We are to dare to believe and act upon the faith promise of Romans 4:17 where we call those things which do not exist as though they did.

__T__ 2. You become what you believe.

workbook

chapter four
"more than enough for your healing"

Part 1. Please complete the following statements using the text as your guide.

1. El Shaddai "is able to do exceedingly abundantly above all that we ask or think, according to the _power_ that works in us" (Ephesians 3:20).

2. El Shaddai is portrayed in Scripture as a God of abounding, unending love and goodness, who wants to give good gifts to His children. "Every _good_ gift and every _perfect_ gift is from above, and comes down from the Father of lights, with whom there is no variation or shadow of turning" (James 1:17).

3. Jesus was anointed with dunamis power for what four (4) purposes:
   a. _Preach the gospel to the poor_
   b. _Heal the brokenhearted_
   c. _Preach deliverance to the captives & recovery of sight to the blind_
   d. _Set at liberty those who are oppressed_

4. God promises full life to His children. "With _long_ _life_ I will satisfy him, and show him My salvation" (Psalm 91:16).

5. The only condition set forth in God's Word to receive God's healing virtue is to develop a __loving__ relationship with Him.

6. When we do what God's Word says, we open the door for His __Blessings__ to flow.

7. Sickness came into the world by the __disobedience__ of man.

8. Christ's mission is recorded in the following three (3) Scriptures:

Isaiah 53:4-5

"Surely He has borne our griefs and carried our sorrows; yet we esteemed Him stricken, smitten by God, and afflicted. But He was wounded for our __transgressions__, He was bruised for our __iniquities__; the chastisement for our peace was upon Him, and by His __stripes__ we are healed."

Matthew 8:17:

"That it might be fulfilled which was spoken by Isaiah the prophet, saying: 'He Himself took our __infirmities__ and bore our __sicknesses__.'"

1 Peter 2:24:

"Who Himself bore our __sins__ in His own body on the tree, that we, having died to sins, might live for righteousness—by whose __stripes__ you were healed."

9. Please list the three (3) major steps that were given to receive what God has provided for you:

a. __God wants to heal me__

b. __I must want God to heal me.__

c. _I must claim healing by the Promise!_

10. God's desire for His children (for you) is clearly expressed in 3 John 2. "Beloved, I pray that you may __prosper__ in all things and be in __health__, just as your soul prospers."

Part 2. TRUE OR FALSE: Please put a T in the blank if the statement is True; F if the statement is False.

__T__ 1. From Genesis to Revelation, the Bible proclaims the story of God's healing power.

__T__ 2. Sickness is not a gift of God.

__T__ 3. Our health and healing has already been bought and paid for.

chapter five
"more than enough for your family"

Part 1. Please complete the following statements using the text as your guide.

1. When it is working as the Lord intended, the _family_ provides for virtually every need of its individual members.

2. Satan viciously attacks the family, because it is the living embodiment of God's _love_ to mankind and provides a source of _strength_ and _protection_ against all outside forces.

3. The first time God revealed Himself as El Shaddai in Genesis, it was to pronounce a promise of _blessing_ upon the family of Abram.

4. Jesus had a difficult time ministering to His family and neighbors.

   "Then He [Jesus] went out from there and came to His own country ... now He could do no _mighty works_ there, except that He laid His hands on a few sick people and healed them. And He marveled because of their _unbelief_" (Mark 6:1, 5-6).

5. Jesus also said, "... A prophet is not without honor except in his _own_ country and among his _own_ relatives, and in his _own_ house" (Mark 6:4).

6. The unsaved might not receive you, because darkness is not comfortable in the presence of _light_.

workbook

7. God promises us many times in His Word that if we are __obedient__ to Him, He will save our families. Some of the Scriptures which reinforce this truth are:

   Psalm 103:17—"But the mercy of the Lord is from everlasting to everlasting on those who fear Him, and His righteousness to children's __children__."

   Proverbs 11:21—"The posterity of the righteous will be __delivered__."

   Isaiah 44:3—"I will pour My Spirit on your __descendants__, and My blessing on your __offspring__."

   Isaiah 49:25—"For I will contend with him who contends with you, and I will __save__ your children."

   Acts 16:31—"__Believe__ on the Lord Jesus Christ, and you will be saved, __you__ and __your__ household."

8. God is "... not willing that any should __perish__, but that all should come to __repentance__" (2 Peter 3:9).

9. True repentance means turning around and going in another __direction__.

10. Your persistent __prayers__ on your family's behalf and a daily, consistent __walk__ with God will bring them to Christ.

11. The key to winning your family to Christ is continuing __obedience__ to God's will and unwavering __faith__ in God's Word.

more than enough

12. God spoke through Moses, "I call heaven and earth as witnesses today against you, that I have set before you life and death, blessing and cursing; therefore choose life, that both you and __your__ __descendants__ may live" (Deuteronomy 30:19).

13. God gives Scriptural guidelines to parents in Ephesians 6:4 and Proverbs 22:6 for raising children:

    Ephesians 6:4, AMP.

    "Fathers, do not irritate and provoke your children to __anger__—do not exasperate them to __resentment__—but rear them [__tenderly__] in the __training__ and __discipline__ and the __counsel__ and __admonition__ of the Lord."

    Proverbs 22:6

    "__Train__ up a child in the way he should go, and when he is old he will __not__ depart from it."

14. A vital part of Christian training in the home must be by __example__ as well as by instruction.

15. God commands parents to raise their children to know Him "Therefore you shall lay up these __words__ of mine in your heart and in your soul, and __bind__ them as a sign on your hand, and they shall be as frontlets between your eyes. You shall __teach__ them to your children, __speaking__ of them when you sit in your house, when you __walk__ by the way, when you __lie down__, and when you

rise up. And you shall _write_ them on the doorposts of your house and on your gates, that your days and the days of your _children_ may be multiplied" (Deuteronomy 11:18-21).

16. A good Scripture promise to claim for wayward children who have left home is Isaiah 43:5-6:

    "Fear not, for I am with you; I will bring your _descendants_ from the east, and gather you from the west; I will say to the north, 'Give them up!' and to the south, 'Do not keep them back!' Bring My _sons_ from afar, and My _daughters_ from the ends of the earth."

17. As a parent, make a declaration, "As for me and my house, we will _serve_ the Lord" (Joshua 24:15).

18. To effectively reach your lost loved ones, make a commitment to keep Psalm 101:2: "I will walk within my house with a _perfect_ heart."

19. Your _intercession_ and _faithfulness_ will usher in the miraculous for your family and friends. Your _steadfastness_ is their key to receiving salvation.

Part 2. TRUE OR FALSE: Please put a T in the blank if the statement is True; F if the statement is False.

_T_ 1. God has provided for the protection and preservation of the family.

_T_ 2. The family relationship gives life its richest meaning.

chapter six
"more than enough for your finances"

Part 1. Please complete the following statements using the text as your guide.

1. It pleases God to bless His children. Psalm 35:27 says, "Let the Lord be magnified, who has pleasure in the __Prosperity__ of His servant." Luke 12:32 says, "Do not fear, little flock, for it is your Father's __good__ __pleasure__ to give you the kingdom."

2. Real prosperity begins in the __soul__.

3. God's prosperity relates to more than finances. Please name six (6) additional areas to which His prosperity applies.

   a. __your relationships__
   b. __your home__
   c. __your marriage__
   d. __your job__
   e. __your health__
   f. __your spiritual life__

4. There is a workable faith for finance, and it is found in __God's Word__.

workbook

5. "Do not be deceived, God is not mocked; for whatever a man ___sows___, that he will also ___reap___" (Galatians 6:7).

6. ___Jesus___ was the greatest giver the world has ever known.

7. Jesus was a ___steward___ of the resources God made available to Him.

8. God promises to meet our needs ___now___ ... in this time.

9. The secret of receiving is giving in faith. Jesus said, "___Give___, and it will be given to you: ___good measure___, ___pressed down___, ___shaken together___, and ___running over___ will be put into your bosom. For with the same measure that you use, it will be measured back to you" (Luke 6:38).

10. Malachi 3:10-11 gives us guidelines regarding our finances. "Bring all the ___tithes___ into the storehouse, that there may be food in My house, and ___prove___ me now in this, says the Lord of hosts, 'If I will not open for you the ___windows of heaven___ and pour out for you such a ___blessing___ that there will not be room enough to receive it. And I will ___rebuke___ the ___devourer___ for your sakes, so that he will not destroy the fruit of your ground, nor shall the vine fail to bear fruit for you in the field,' says the Lord of hosts."

11. When you give God your best, He gives back His ___best___ to you.

12. The only place in all of the Bible we are told to test God is in regard to His ___reward___ for our giving.

Part 2. TRUE OR FALSE: Please put a T in the blank if the statement is True; F if the statement is False.

___T___ 1. God is not a vending machine that delivers any item you want if you put enough coins in the slot and push the right button. Neither is He so limited or stingy that He reluctantly doles out just enough to keep you going.

workbook

chapter seven
"more than enough for your weaknesses"

Part 1. Please complete the following statements using the text as your guide.

1. By drawing upon the strength of El Shaddai, you can __Conquer__ every challenge and __overcome__ every weakness.

2. __Fear__ is the most common crippler of the inner man. __Fear__ is the enemy of faith.

3. God's Word says, "Perfect __love__ casts out fear."

4. Ephesians 6:10 says we are to be strong in __the Lord__.

5. Second Timothy 1:7 says, "For God has not given us a spirit of fear, but of __power__ and of __love__ and of a __sound mind__."

6. While the thief (Satan) offers you each of the following negatives, list the corresponding positives which Jesus offers:

   Satan's Negatives   Jesus' Positives

   a. Fear   __Faith__

   b. Sickness   __Healing__

   c. Loneliness   __Hope__

more than enough

    d. Hopelessness   _Belonging_

    e. Poverty   _Prosperity_

    f. Turmoil   _Peace_

    g. Sorrow   _Joy_

    h. Hate   _Love_

7. Guilt consciousness prevails in the church world because of misinterpretations of the laws of _Cause_ and _effect_ and of the _Nature_ of God.

8. Many lives are unfulfilled and unsettled because of _Guilt_ (real or imagined).

9. El Shaddai—the God of more than enough—offers you pardon, mercy, and release from all of Satan's _bondage_.

10. Christ's forgiveness frees us from the guilt and death penalty of sin. "There is therefore now no _Condemnation_ to those who are in Christ Jesus, who do not walk according to the flesh, but according to the _Spirit_."

11. Christians are never alone, for Jesus said, "I am with you _always_."

12. The peace of God "… which surpasses all understanding, will _guard_ your hearts and minds through Christ Jesus" (Philippians 4:7).

13. God has promised peace for all of His children. "_Peace_ I leave with you, My _peace_ I give to you: not as the

world gives do I give to you. Let not your heart be __troubled__, neither let it be __afraid__" (John 14:27).

14. One of the best ways to be completely free of loneliness is to become interested in the welfare of __others__.

15. God's promise in Luke 10:19 is for every believer. "Behold, I give you the __authority__ to trample on serpents and scorpions, and over __all__ the power of the enemy, and __nothing__ shall by any means hurt you."

16. We can say as David said, "The Lord is the __strength__ of my life; of whom shall I be afraid?" (Psalm 27:1).

Part 2. TRUE OR FALSE: Please put a T in the blank if the statement is True; F if the statement is False.

__T__ 1. In Christ Jesus is the strength and courage you need to rise above the discouragement that accompanies loneliness.

more than enough

chapter eight
"more than enough for your circumstances"

Part 1. Please complete the following statements using the text as your guide.

1. Paul, like the mother eagle and her eaglets, learned to live above the circumstances and storms of life. "Do not think that I am saying this under pressure of want. For I, however I am placed, have learned to be ___independent___ of circumstances. I know how to face ___humble___ circumstances, and I know how to face ___prosperity___. Into all and every human experience I have been initiated—into plenty and hunger, into prosperity and want. I can do ___everything___ in the strength of him who makes me strong" (Philippians 4:11-13), 20th Century New Testament).

2. According to John 10:10, it is Satan who comes to ___kill___, ___steal___, and ___destroy___, while Jesus came that we might have life and have it ___more abundantly___.

3. To handle the irritants that enter our lives, we should wrap our ___faith___ in God around the problems and watch God work.

4. Six (6) of the Scriptures that I held to in time of change in my life are:

    a. Deuteronomy 31:6—"Be ___strong___ and of ___good courage___, do not ___fear___

workbook

nor be afraid of them; for the Lord your God, He is the One who goes with you. He will not leave you nor forsake you.

b. Matthew 6:33—"But seek first the _kingdom of_ _God_ and _His_ _righteousness_, and all these things shall be added to you."

c. Mark 11:23-24—"For assuredly, I say to you, whoever _says_ to this mountain, 'Be removed and be cast into the sea,' and does not _doubt_ in his heart, but _believes_ that those things he says will come to pass, he will have whatever he says. Therefore I say to you, whatever things you ask when you pray, _believe_ that you _receive_ them, and you will have them."

d. Luke 1:37—"For with God _nothing_ will be impossible."

e. Proverbs 3:5-6—"_Trust_ in the Lord with all your heart, and lean not on your own understanding: in all your ways _acknowledge Him_, and He shall _direct_ your paths."

f. Psalm 37:5—"_Commit_ your way to the Lord, _trust_ also in Him, and He shall bring it to pass."

5. You can stand on God's promise in Romans 8:28—"And we know that all things work together for good to those who _love_ God, to those who are the _called_ according to His purpose."

6. We can be like Paul in every situation we face:

    Philippians 4:4-9:

    "Rejoice in the Lord _always_. Again I will say, rejoice!

    "Let your _gentleness_ be known to all men. The Lord is at hand.

    "Be anxious for nothing, but in everything by _prayer_ and _supplication_, with _thanksgiving_, let your requests be made known to God;

    "And the _peace_ of God which surpasses all understanding, will _guard_ your hearts and minds through Christ Jesus.

    "Finally, brethren, whatever things are _true_, whatever things are _noble_, whatever things are _just_, whatever things are _pure_, whatever things are _lovely_, whatever things are of _good report_, if there is any _virtue_ and if there is anything _praiseworthy_—meditate on these things.

    "The things which you learned and received and heard and saw in me, these do, and the God of peace will be with you."

7. To achieve victory over every circumstance, we are to "… hold fast the _confession_ of our hope without _wavering_, for He who promised is faithful" (Hebrews 10:23).

Part 2. TRUE OR FALSE: Please put a T in the blank if the statement is True; F if the statement is False.

__T__ 1. El Shaddai is more than enough to give you victory over every circumstance, every disappointment, or every loss you may have experienced.

__T__ 2. God is always true to His Word.

chapter nine
"more than enough for your every need"

Part 1. Please complete the following statements using the text as your guide.

1. One of my favorite "blank-check" promises is John 15:7: "If you ___abide___ in Me, and My words ___abide___ in you, you will ask what you desire, and it shall ___be done___ _____ for you."

2. According to Mrs. Reedy's translation, if what you need isn't in stock or doesn't exist, God will ___create___ the thing you need and cause your desired situations to come to pass.

3. The abundant blessings of El Shaddai go far beyond the absolute ___needs___ and ___necessities___ of life.

4. As God's children, we don't have to settle for a "minimum" survival. We can enjoy God's best.
"___Trust___ in the Lord, and do good; dwell in the land, and feed on His faithfulness. ___Delight___ yourself also in the Lord, and He shall give you the desires of your heart. ___Commit___ your way to the Lord, trust also in Him, and He shall bring it to pass" (Psalm 37:3-5).

5. A covenant is an ___agreement___ or contract.

6. If you are "... ___willing___ and ___obedient___, you shall eat the good of the land" (Isaiah 1:19).

workbook

7. David said, "Those who seek the Lord shall not __lack__ any good thing" (Psalm 34:10).

8. __Abundance__ should be a way of life for the believer.

9. Second Peter 1:3 says we, as believers, have been given __all__ _____ things that pertain to life and godliness.

10. The word "all" is nestled in the middle of several of God's promises. Here are three such examples:

    a. Psalm 103:3—"… Who forgives __all__ your iniquities, who heals __all__ your diseases."

    b. Philippians 4:19—"And my God shall supply __all__ your need according to His riches in glory by Christ Jesus."

    c. Matthew 28:18—"__All__ authority has been given to Me in heaven and on earth."

11. __Obedience__ brings abundance. __Labor__ brings blessings. __Perseverance__ brings results.

12. Second Corinthians 9:8 is a beautiful promise for all believers: "God is able to make all __things__ abound toward you, that you, always having __all sufficiency__ in all things, have an abundance for every good work."

Part 2. TRUE OR FALSE: Please put a T in the blank if the statement is True; F if the statement is False.

__T__ 1. Jesus, revealing the El Shaddai nature of God, turned water into wine.

___T___ 2. Jesus displayed the El Shaddai nature of God again when He miraculously multiplied five loaves of bread and two fish to provide food for 5,000 men, plus women and children.

___T___ 3. God will never go back on His Word.

workbook

chapter ten
"releasing the power of El Shaddai"

Part 1. Please complete the following statements using the text as your guide

1. The fullness of God's power is not released without __action__. __Obeying__ God is the key to releasing the power of El Shaddai.

2. God delights in the prosperity of His children. "Let the Lord be magnified, who has __pleasure__ in the prosperity of His servant" (Psalm 35:27).

3. God desires that you "... __prosper__ in all things and be in __health__, just as your soul prospers" (3 John 2).

4. I am the Lord your God who __teaches__ you to profit, who __leads__ you by the way you should go" (Isaiah 48:17).

5. Please list the eight (8) steps or keys given to release the power of El Shaddai.

   a. __Believe the abundant life is God's will for you.__
   b. __Discover the work God has called you to do.__
   c. __Have faith in God.__
   d. __Establish a partnership w/ God.__
   e. __Be Bold to launch out in new ventures__
   f. __Obey the Golden rule__

g. _Put God first_
h. _Pay your tithes & put God to the test._

6. God's Word is His will and it contains more than __1000__ promises for your well-being and spiritual abundance.

7. The key to achieving God's best is to develop your __faith__ to rock-hard consistency.

8. Solomon said in Proverbs 10:22, "The blessing of the Lord makes one __rich__, and He adds no sorrow to it."

9. When you let God have everything you have, He gives you access to everything He has. "Give, and it will be given to you: good measure, pressed down, shaken together, and running over will be put into your bosom. For with the __measure__ that you use, it will be measured back to you" (Luke 6:38).

10. It is a spiritual principle that we are to honor the Lord with our possessions and with the __firstfruits__ of all our increase. In this way, Solomon says, "… Your barns will be filled with __plenty__, and your vats will __overflow__ with new wine." (Proverbs 3:9).

11. Paul said if we sow sparingly, we will reap __sparingly__, but if we sow bountifully, we will reap __bountifully__ (2 Corinthians 9:6).

12. God loves a __cheerful__ giver (2 Corinthians 9:7).

Part 2. TRUE OR FALSE: Please put a T in the blank if the statement is True; F if the statement is False.

__T__ 1. The Holy Spirit is never out of control.

"Goodbye. I'll see you here…there… or in the air."

VICKI JAMISON-PETERSON
1936-2008

Made in the USA
San Bernardino, CA
24 December 2014